Divorce the Collaborative Way.
Is It the Way For You?

MELINDA EITZEN, JD,
SCOTT CLARKE, CFP &
VICKI JAMES, MS, LPC, LMFT

iUniverse books may be ordered through booksellers or by contacting:

iUniverse
1663 Liberty Drive
Bloomington, IN 47403
www.iuniverse.com
1-800-Authors (1-800-288-4677)

ISBN: 978-1-4401-5466-9 (sc)
ISBN: 978-1-4401-5467-6 (e)

Print information available on the last page.

iUniverse rev. date: 04/12/2019

Contents

About the Authors

Melinda Eitzen, recently recognized by D Magazine as one of the "Best Lawyers in Dallas" and one of the "Best Family Law Mediators in Dallas", is an attorney on the forefront of the collaborative law movement in Texas, is a partner in the Dallas-Fort Worth area-based family law practice of Duffee + Eitzen. Melinda has served as President of the Collin County Bar Association and as a Member of the Board of Directors of Texas Lawyers for Children from 2011-2013, as President of the **Plano Bar Association**, as a chair of the Collaborative Law Alliance of Collin County, Vice President of the Collin County Bar Association, chair of the Good Works Committee of the Collin County Bar Association, director of the Dallas Association of Young Lawyers, director of Texas Young Lawyers Association, and chair of the Family Law Section of the Collin County Bar Association. You can contact Melinda by calling 214-416-9010 or by emailing her at melinda@d-elaw.com. For more information about Duffee& Eitzen, go to d-elaw.com.

Scott Clarke is a Certified Financial Planner and Certified Divorce Financial Analyst in private practice in the Dallas-Fort Worth area. He currently serves on the Board of Trustees of the Collaborative Law Institute of Texas and provides training to other financial professionals on the role of the financial neutral in collaborative divorce in Texas and throughout the country. Scott can be reached by phone at 817-685-7570 or at scott@clarkefg.com.

Vicki M. James is a Licensed Professional Counselor and a Licensed Marriage and Family Therapist in Dallas. Vicki works as a team member in collaborative divorces helping to facilitate communication. She is a member of the Collaborative Law Institute of Texas and of the International Association of Collaborative Professionals, where she is on the Civil Law Committee. Vicki is also a member of the Texas Collaborative Law Council, Inc. Get in touch with Vicki by going to www.vmjames.com, e-mailing her at vmjames@sbcglobal.net, or calling her at 214-361-8771.

Chapter#1, You're Getting Divorced. Now What?

When you and your spouse were preparing to get married, your relationship was all about romance and planning your future together. The biggest decisions you may have had to make were where the two of you would live once you were married, where you would store all of your wedding gifts, and how soon you would begin a family. Making those decisions was easy because the two of you were able to communicate and cooperate with one another.

Now that you're getting divorced, you and your spouse face a whole host of much more complex decisions, like how you will divvy up the assets and debts from your marriage and whether one of you will pay spousal support to the other. If you have minor children together (children who are younger than age 18), you'll also have to decide how you'll handle their custody, visitation and support and the role that any extended family members who are currently in your children's lives will play after your divorce. If you're like most divorcing couples, making these decisions won't be easy because feelings like sadness, anger, hurt, regret, and disappointment will have replaced the love you once felt for one another, making communication and cooperation difficult if not impossible for the two of you.

Given the challenges ahead it's important for you to know that in Texas there is more than one way to get divorced and that the particular process you choose can have a big impact, for better or worse, on the final terms of your divorce. It can also affect how difficult your divorce will be for you and your family emotionally, how much support you will have as you go through the process, and how prepared you will be for your life after divorce. Also, if you and your spouse have young children together, the divorce method you choose is likely to have a great effect on your ability to do a good job of co-parenting them post-divorce.

Your getting divorced options are:

- Do your own divorce
- Get a litigated divorce
- Pursue a collaborative divorce

This chapter in *Divorce the Collaborative Way. Is It the Way For You?* introduces you to these three divorce alternatives and also provides general explanations of how they each work. However, as the title of this book suggests, the rest of the chapters focus on the collaborative divorce process specifically because as divorce professionals, we believe that it's the superior way for most married couples to end their marriage. As you read *Divorce the Collaborative Way*, our reasons for thinking this way will become clear.

Do Your Own Divorce

If you and your spouse decide to do your own divorce, you'll work out the terms of your settlement agreement and file all of the legally required paperwork on your own without the help of attorneys. (In a variation of this arrangement, some couples do their own negotiating and then one of them hires an attorney who formalizes everything by drafting the appropriate legal documents.) Doing your own divorce has its advantages and disadvantages. Its primary advantages are:

- You'll minimize your involvement with the legal system.
- Your divorce will not cost a lot because you won't incur any attorney fees or expenses other than a court filing fee of between $350 and $400.
- You and your spouse will have complete control over your divorce, including deciding when, where and how you'll work out the terms of your settlement agreement.

The key disadvantages of a do-it-yourself divorce include:

- You won't have an attorney by your side to explain the intricacies of the law, to negotiate for you, to look out for your best interests, and to help you avoid costly mistakes.

- If you aren't fully informed about your family's finances, don't understand your legal rights, or if your spouse is a much better negotiator than you are, you may not get what you are entitled to in your divorce and you may agree to terms that are legally unenforceable.
- If your experience mirrors that of many other people who try to do their own divorce, you and your spouse will abandon your do-it-yourself efforts eventually and hire attorneys.

When a Do-It-Yourself Divorce is Not a Good Idea

Even attempting to do your own divorce is a foolhardy idea if:

- You and your spouse can't have a calm, non-emotional conversation about the issues in your divorce. If that's the case, your efforts to work out the terms of your divorce will be little more than an exercise in frustration and futility.
- You and your spouse have trouble communicating with one another. For example, you can't get your points across and/or your spouse constantly interrupts you.
- You and your spouse are unwilling to consider one another's points of view and to compromise with each other. In order to have a successful negotiation, you must be open to taking each other's points of view into account.
- You're easily manipulated by your spouse or your spouse is abusive to you. Under such circumstances doing your own divorce is a recipe for disaster.
- You know little or nothing about your family's finances. If you are unfamiliar with what you and your spouse own and owe as a couple, you're likely to end up on the "short end of the stick" financially.
- Your marital estate includes complicated assets, like stocks and mutual funds, investment real estate, pensions, other retirement assets, or business interests.
- You and your spouse are unable to agree on how to share parenting time.

Get a Litigated Divorce

A litigated divorce is a complicated, adversarial legal process that involves attorneys, legal procedures, court hearings, settlement efforts, and maybe even a trial and that pits one spouse against the other in a win-lose battle. For example, if you opt for a litigated divorce, your attorney may make disparaging comments about your spouse in an effort to provoke and discredit him and may try to wear him down emotionally and financially by filing a lot of legal motions and scheduling multiple court hearings. Your spouse's attorney may try to do the same to you. As a result, the bad feelings between you and your spouse will probably become more intense as time goes on and so achieving a negotiated settlement will become increasingly difficult and expensive.

If you and your spouse become so estranged from one another and so entrenched in your positions that your attorneys' negotiations get you no where, your divorce will go to trial. Should that happen you'll lose all control over the terms of your divorce, the cost of your divorce will skyrocket, and your divorce will become even more emotionally difficult and damaging.

Warning! Although most divorces headed for trial are settled either before the trial begins or once it's underway, by the time that happens you and your spouse will have already "gone through the ringer" emotionally and you'll have paid your attorneys a lot of money to prepare for the trial. Also, your children may be emotionally harmed by the adversarial nature of the trial preparation process.

How a Litigated Divorce Works

A litigated divorce begins when the attorney for one spouse files with the court an *Original Petition for Divorce* on behalf of that spouse (For purposes of discussion, let's assume that your attorney is the one who files the petition.) The petition provides information about you and your spouse and your marriage, among other things. When your attorney files the petition you are actually initiating a divorce lawsuit against your spouse, which means that you become the *petitioner* in the lawsuit and your spouse becomes the *respondent*.

As the respondent, your spouse is entitled to file a formal, written *answer* (or response) to the information in your petition.

A 60-day waiting period begins after the petition has been filed. Even though the waiting period gives you and your spouse an opportunity to decide if you really want to end your marriage, your attorneys will begin gathering the information they need to work out the terms of your divorce during that time. Most of the information will relate to your family's finances -- what you and your spouse own and owe (your marital assets and debts), your individual incomes, your projected monthly post-divorce budgets, and so on; but the attorneys will talk to potential witnesses and may also gather information about your individual parenting skills, health status, lifestyles, and so on. They will pull together most of the information they need using the tools of the formal discovery process, which are described later in this chapter in Figure 1.1, *Tools of Formal Discovery.*

The attorneys will also obtain information by asking you and your spouse to complete *Sworn Inventory and Appraisement* forms, which ask you to list all of your marital debts and their amounts and all of your marital assets and their market or current values. If you and your spouse disagree about the value of a particular asset, you may each hire your own outside expert to help you make that determination. If the experts' information does not end your dispute, the issue will be considered at a court hearing and a judge will decide what the asset is worth.

Warning! The more formal discovery there is in your divorce, the more outside experts you hire, and the more hearings there are, the more costly and time consuming your divorce will be.

If there are interim issues in your divorce that you or your spouse want resolved immediately while the final terms of your divorce are being worked out, both attorneys will file temporary motions with the court. For example, you may want the right to continue living in your family's home while your divorce case is pending, to have primary custody of your children, and to receive temporary spousal and/or child support. Resolving temporary issues in a litigated divorce can be an extremely contentious process and often sets the tone for the rest of a divorce.

Whenever the attorneys are able to negotiate a temporary agreement on an issue, an *agreed order* is filed with the court and everything in the order becomes legally enforceable once the judge signs it. If the attorneys are not able to negotiate a temporary agreement on a particular issue, a court hearing is scheduled and a judge rules on the issue after the hearing.

Warning! When you let the court decide an issue in your divorce you have no guarantee that you'll be happy with its decision.

Once the attorneys have all of the information they need, they will try to negotiate the final terms of your divorce based on the letter of the law. Your attorney will keep you informed of any offers or counter offers your spouse may make to you through his attorney, will discuss any offers or counter offers you may want to make to your spouse, and will let you know about any problems that may develop during the negotiation process.

Warning! Your attorney should not sign off on anything related to the final terms of your divorce without your permission.

The two attorneys may be able to work out the final terms of your divorce within the 60-day waiting period, but it's likely that their negotiations will take much longer -- between three and six months in most divorces. Exactly how long will depend among other things on the number and complexity of the issues the two attorneys are trying to resolve, the amount of discovery in your divorce, how willing you and your spouse are to compromise with one another, the number of motions and hearings in your divorce, and how aggressive the attorneys are. Aggressive attorneys are more apt to file a lot of motions and use other adversarial legal tactics to get their clients the divorce agreement they want.

Warning! If you want your divorce to be amicable, but your spouse hires an aggressive attorney, you'll probably feel like you need to hire that kind of attorney too so that you can "fight fire with fire." As a result, your divorce will be anything but friendly.

If you and your spouse have minor children, other factors may affect the length of your litigated divorce. For example, if the two of you cannot agree on how to handle the custody of your children, a *social study* may be conducted, which involves a social worker meeting with you and your spouse and your children, coming to your home, talking with your children's teachers, friends, babysitters, and other third parties, and possibly reviewing relevant records, like your children's medical and school records, for example. The study results provide insight into your children's parenting needs and the ability of you and your spouse to meet them. In addition, psychological evaluations of you and/or your spouse and possibly your children too may also be conducted if someone requests them and if the court believes that the evaluations would be advisable. The psychological evaluations, which are conducted by a psychologist, usually a Ph.D. or a psychiatrist, objectively determine whether you and/or your spouse have any mental health disorders, which could affect your ability to do a good job of parenting your children.

Jim and Lauren Braxton have been married for 15 years and have four young children. For the past seven years, Jim has struggled with a drug problem. A couple months ago, Lauren finally got fed up with Jim's problem and filed for divorce. Not long after she took that step, Jim went into rehab and Lauren's attorney subsequently filed a motion for temporary orders asking the court to prohibit Jim from spending any time alone with his children because of his drug problem. The motion also alleged that Jim had been physically abusive to Lauren during their marriage.

During the court hearing on the motion, Lauren's attorney tried to prove the abuse by introducing into evidence a letter that Jim had written to Lauren shortly after he went into rehab. Jim had bared his soul in the letter, including admitting to the physical abuse. He also apologized for all of the mistakes he had made during their marriage.

Jim was totally surprised that Lauren had shared his letter with her attorney. It was obvious from the look on his face while the letter was being read aloud that he was devastated that Lauren would allow her attorney to use his heart-felt comments to get her what she wanted in their divorce. Jim felt totally betrayed by his wife and decided that he could no longer trust her.

What happened at the hearing set the tone for the rest of the couple's divorce. Although Jim had wanted to keep everything friendly because he felt guilty for what his drug problems had done to his marriage, he stopped feeling that way because of Lauren's actions. As a result, the couple's divorce was very difficult and now that it's over, Jim and Lauren's relationship is contentious and they fight constantly about their two kids.

Figure 1.1, The Tools of Formal Discovery

Attorneys involved in a litigated divorce use different legal tools during the formal discovery process to gather the information that they need to help their clients. Those tools are:

- *Deposition.* If you are deposed by your spouse's attorney, he will ask you a series of questions outside of court -- probably in your attorney's office --that you will have to answer under oath. Some of the attorney's questions may be intended to make you feel uncomfortable, upset you, confuse you, or discredit you. A court reporter will create a written record of everything that you say and a videographer may also create a visual record of your answers. The court reporter's transcript and the videotape may be used as evidence in your divorce. Your attorney will be by your side throughout the deposition and you'll be able to stop the process whenever you want to ask her questions. Your attorney may also depose your spouse and both attorneys may depose other people who they believe have information related to your divorce, like your family's CPA, financial planner, your paramours if you or your spouse have been unfaithful to one another, your children's babysitters, childcare providers and teachers, your doctors and mental health therapists, your business partners, close friends, and family members.
- *Interrogatory.* An interrogatory is a set of written questions that your spouse's attorney may ask you to answer in writing and/or that your attorney may ask your spouse to answer.
- *Request for production of documents.* This is a formal written request for specific documents and records, like your bank records and tax returns, earnings statements, deeds to your real estate, titles to your vehicles, loan agreements you've

signed, credit card statements, statements related to your investments, cell phone records, and so on. You and your spouse may each have to produce documents, as may others like your employer, CPA, financial planner, banker, broker, and so on.

If the Attorneys Are Able to Settle All of the Issues in Your Divorce

If you and your spouse and the two attorneys are able to resolve all of the issues in your divorce, the attorneys will prepare a draft settlement agreement that reflects everything you and your spouse have agreed to. You and your spouse will review the draft and may ask for changes. It may take several rounds of reviews and revisions before you have a final agreement, or *agreed decree of divorce.*

Once you have a final agreement, you and your spouse will sign it and then you and your attorney or your spouse and his attorney -- it's usually the petitioner and her attorney -- will go to court and *enter* the decree. After the judge signs it, your divorce becomes official.

Warning! If your divorce is prolonged and difficult, you may agree to a settlement even if you aren't happy with its terms because you can't afford to keep negotiating and/or go to trial or because you're emotionally worn out and want your divorce to be over.

If the Attorneys Can't Reach an Agreement

If you and your spouse and the two attorneys are unable to negotiate a divorce agreement that's acceptable to both of you, the lawyers will probably suggest that you and your spouse try to work out your differences by attending mediation, which is a non-court dispute resolution method. Figure 1.2 *How Mediation Works* provides a brief explanation of the process.

Warning! If you ask the court for a trial date without having tried mediation, the judge may refuse to give you a date until you do.

If you or your spouse refuse to try mediation or if the two of you do try it and it doesn't end your stalemate, one of the attorneys will ask the divorce court in your area for a trial date. Depending on how busy the court is, the trial could be scheduled for months later. At the trial, both attorneys will present all of their evidence and question witnesses (including you and your spouse) in order to try to make a convincing case for their clients. Then the judge (or a jury if you and your spouse asked for a jury trial) will decide the issues in your divorce based on the evidence presented.

Warning! Due to court-imposed deadlines, your attorney will probably have to begin preparing for the possibility of a trial at the very same time that she is trying to negotiate a settlement in your divorce. However, given that an estimated 85% of all divorces are resolved outside of court, it's very likely that you'll pay your attorney for services you never need.

Figure 1.2, How Mediation Works

Mediation is a non-court dispute resolution process. If you and your spouse go to mediation, a trained, neutral mediator, who may be an attorney, will facilitate the process by helping the two of you stay focused on the issues you're trying to resolve, communicate productively, brainstorm solutions, and compromise with one another. The mediator will not do the negotiating for you, side with you or your spouse, tell you what you should or shouldn't decide, or offer you legal advice. In other words, the mediator will not be a decision maker, but merely a settlement facilitator.

During mediation you and your attorney will be in one room and your spouse and his attorney will be in a different room most likely. The mediator will shuttle back and forth between the two rooms, conveying any offers and counter offers you and your spouse may make to one another and letting each of you know where there may be room for compromise. You'll be able to consult with your attorney throughout the process.

Pursue a Collaborative Divorce

The Texas legislature amended the Family Code in 2001 to give divorcing couples in this state the option of getting a collaborative divorce. A collaborative divorce is a highly structured, non-adversarial, non-court process that helps couples identify mutually-acceptable solutions to the issues in their divorce, protect their families, if they have minor children, and end their marriages with integrity and with their dignity intact.

If you and your spouse decide to pursue a collaborative divorce you will each hire your own collaborative divorce attorneys, who will have received extensive training in the collaborative process and with their help and guidance, the two of you together will also hire a neutral mental health professional and a neutral financial professional, who will work for both of you. The two neutrals will also have been trained in the collaborative process. The mental health professional will be a licensed counselor or social worker, who specializes in working with families, or a marriage and family therapist. The financial professional will most likely be a certified Financial Planner™ (CFP) or a CPA. The two neutrals together with your attorneys will act as your divorce team -- sort of like your divorce consultants -- providing you and your spouse with guidance, advice, support and ideas.

One of the most important aspects of a collaborative divorce is that everyone agrees up-front that going to court is not an option and that no one will even threaten the other with a court action. Therefore, if you and your spouse opt for a collaborative divorce and later decide that you want to take your divorce to court, under the terms of your agreement your attorneys will have to withdraw from your case and you'll have to hire new attorneys. For this reason, everyone involved in a collaborative divorce is highly motivated to reach a negotiated settlement.

Why Consider a Collaborative Divorce

There are many compelling reasons to end your marriage through a collaborative divorce. For example, the process helps you:

- Protect your children from the harmful effects of divorce and makes it easier for you and your spouse to raise them together once your marriage is officially over. In fact, this is one of the main reasons that parents with young children opt for a collaborative divorce.

- Communicate productively with your spouse, even if the two of you can't stand one another anymore.
- Feel good about the way you've ended your marriage. Although going through a divorce is never easy or pleasant, the collaborative process helps you maintain your dignity rather than getting "down in the dirt" as happens in so many litigated divorces. As a result, at the end of your collaborative divorce you're more apt to feel good about the way you conducted yourself and more apt to be friends with your spouse, if that's something that you both want. In fact, in some collaborative divorces, spouses begin the process hating one another and barely able to speak to each other much less look one another in the eyes. Yet, by the time their divorce is over, some of them are talking, smiling and even hugging each other. Of course, other couples who go through the collaborative divorce process are never able to get over their dislike for one another. Even so, with the help of their team, they are still able to negotiate a settlement agreement that is acceptable to both of them.
- Come up with creative solutions to the issues in your divorce that respond to your particular needs and the realities of your life, rather than having to settle for the cookie cutter solutions that tend to be the products of a litigated divorce because of the limitations on what is allowed under the law. In other words, the collaborative process won't limit you and your spouse in terms of possible solutions to the issues in your divorce. For example, in a litigated divorce, the law and therefore the court does not address how ex-spouses should handle the expenses of their children once the children have turned 18 and are out of high school even though the post-high school years can be a very expensive time in a child's life, especially if the child attends college. In a collaborative divorce however, you and your spouse can reach an up-front agreement on how you will handle those expenses.
- Honor the good aspects of your marriage. There are some

positive aspects to nearly every marriage even if the marriage does not work out in the end. For example, you and your spouse may have children from your marriage. The collaborative process allows you to recognize and pay tribute to what is good about your relationship rather than just focusing on all of its problems and shortcomings.

• Move on with your life. The process helps you focus on and plan for your future rather than staying stuck in the problems of your marriage. Many spouses also find the collaborative divorce process to be healing, which makes it easier for them to put their failed marriage behind them and move forward.

Another reason to consider a collaborative divorce is that it makes it less likely that you and your spouse will battle with one another (maybe even in court) over the terms of your divorce agreement once your marriage is officially over. That's because the two of you will have had control over the process and so both of you are more likely to be satisfied with the terms of your divorce agreement. In contrast, if you pursue a litigated divorce you (or your spouse) may feel like you have to accept an agreement that you don't like because of the strategies used by your spouse's attorney, the expense of your divorce, and/or the toll it's taking on your emotions; or your divorce may end in a trial, in which case the conditions of your divorce will be imposed on you.

A Few More Comments About the Collaborative Divorce Process

Although there are many positive aspects to a collaborative divorce, going through the process won't be easy, because you and your spouse will have to sit at the same table and work out the terms of your divorce together even if you are raging mad at one another, distrustful of each other, have not had a civil conversation in months, and are not in the mood for compromise. And, even though you'll have a team of professionals to support and advise you throughout the collaborative divorce process, to help keep the process moving forward and to make sure that everyone stays on task, the process is client-driven. In other words, those professionals cannot do the work of your divorce for you. It will be up to you and your spouse to resolve the issues in your divorce using the problem-solving tools that your team members will give you. Even so, based on our experience working with countless divorcing couples that have used the collaborative divorce process to end their marriages, the process *does* work and tends to produce the best results for families.

Chapter #2, The Features and Benefits of a Collaborative Divorce

This chapter deepens your understanding of the collaborative divorce process by highlighting its key features and benefits and by detailing the differences between a collaborative and a litigated divorce. The chapter also provides a checklist for determining if a collaborative divorce is right for you and a set of commonly asked questions about the collaborative process along with answers to each one.

Understanding What's Unique About a Collaborative Divorce

In a collaborative divorce, the method you use to negotiate the terms of your divorce, the environment within which you conduct your negotiations, your negotiating mindset, the range of options you have for resolving the issues in your divorce, and the kinds of support and assistance you'll receive throughout the process are very different from a litigated divorce. This section explains those differences.

Going to Court is Not an Option

At the very start of your collaborative divorce, you, your spouse and your attorneys will sign a *Participation Agreement*. When you sign it you'll be committing yourselves to negotiating the terms of your divorce rather than going to court -- you'll even be agreeing not to threaten one another with a court action -- and you'll be acknowledging that you understand that if you and your spouse can't settle the issues in your divorce and want the court to decide them for you, your attorneys will withdraw from your case and the two of you will have to hire new attorneys. The *Everyone Will Play By the Same Rules* section later in this chapter discusses the Participation Agreement and you'll find a sample agreement in the appendix to this book.

Going to court is always an option in a litigated divorce. It's the hammer that you and your spouse will hold over one another's heads in order to try to get what you want from your divorce. For example, if your spouse threatens to take you to court you may feel that you have no option but to go along with what he wants from your divorce because you can't afford the cost of a trial and/or because you don't want to experience the emotional stress and strain of a trial.

You and Your Spouse Work Out the Terms of Your Divorce Together

In a collaborative divorce, you and your spouse (not your attorneys alone) will negotiate the terms of your divorce during a series of team meetings (also referred to as joint or collaborative meetings) with the help of your divorce team -- the two attorneys and the neutral mental health and financial professionals. In other words, the two of you will have the leading roles in your divorce and your team members will be the supporting players. In a litigated divorce, the two of you will most likely take a back seat to your attorneys because they will do most of the negotiating for you.

The members of your collaborative divorce team will help you and your spouse reach a negotiated settlement by:

- Explaining the differences between interest-based and positional negotiating and teaching you how to negotiate with your spouse based on your interests. We explain the differences between these two kinds of negotiating in the next section of this book.
- Organizing your negotiations.
- Creating an environment that makes you feel safe stating your opinions, sharing your concerns, and advocating for your own interests during your negotiations. The *You'll Feel Safe* section later in this chapter provides more details about this feature of a collaborative divorce.
- Helping you define and prioritize your divorce interests or goals.

- Ensuring that you have and understand all of the information you need to negotiate the terms of your divorce.
- Helping you brainstorm solutions to the issues in your divorce, evaluate them, and choose the best ones.
- Helping you manage your emotions so they do not get out of control and complicate your divorce.

You Negotiate According to Your Interests, Not Your Positions

Normally in our society we resolve our disputes through a process referred to as *position-based bargaining*, which involves each party in a dispute staking out a position on the issue they disagree about and then doing whatever they can to advance that position. This is how it's done in a litigated divorce.

Here is a silly, simplistic example of how position-based bargaining works: *Susie and Bob Shaw are involved in a litigated divorce. They both want to exit their marriage with the only orange that is growing on the orange tree in their backyard. In other words, they have both taken the position that they want the orange. As a result, in their divorce, one of them will lose -- not get the orange -- and one of them will win -- get the orange.*

There are some serious drawbacks associated with position-based negotiating, including:

- It tends to inflame the emotions of the parties to a dispute, making it more difficult for them to resolve their differences and increasing the likelihood that they will end up in court.
- It causes the parties to become more entrenched in their opinions and less willing to appreciate each other's points of view, which makes compromise difficult, if not impossible.
- It fosters a win-lose mindset, i.e., if I am going to win, you must lose, when in fact there may be a way for both parties to be "winners".

In a collaborative divorce, you negotiate the terms of your divorce according to your interests (your individual interests, the interests you and your spouse may share with one another, and the interests of any young children you may have) rather than your positions. Your interests represent the needs you want to satisfy through your divorce agreement. They are the whys behind your positions. The members of your team will help you define your interests before your negotiations begin. Their help can be invaluable because when you are getting divorced your emotions can make it difficult for you to figure out what you *really* need.

Interest-based negotiating makes it easier for you and your spouse to come up with win-win solutions to the issues in your divorce -- solutions that are acceptable to both of you. Continuing with our orange example, here is how Susie and Bob Shaw might resolve the issue of what to do about the orange on the tree in their backyard if they were getting a collaborative divorce: *The members of their divorce team ask Susie and Bob to explain why they want the orange -- to state their interests in the orange, in other words. Bob says he wants the orange so he can eat it, while Susie says she wants it so that she can use the orange rind in a cake she is going to bake. After identifying their interests in the orange, Bob and Susie are able to identify a solution that satisfies them both -- Bob will get all of the orange pulp and juice and Susie will get all of the orange rind.*

Figure 2.1. further illustrates the differences between the two different approaches to bargaining by providing examples of statements you might make about a particular issue in your divorce depending on whether you were trying to resolve it according to your positions or your interests.

Figure 2.1, Position-Based Versus Interest-based Statements

The following statements help illustrate how you would frame the same issue depending on whether you were resolving it through position-based or interest-based negotiating.

Issue #1, Spousal Support

Position-based statement: I want my husband to pay me $4,000/month after we are divorced.

Interest-based statement: After we are divorced, I would like financial help from my husband so that I can upgrade my job skills and qualify for a well-paying job.

Issue #2, Time With Your Children

Position-based statement: I want custody of our children.

Interest-based statement: I want to continue to be actively involved in the lives of our children day-to-day and to spend a meaningful amount of time with each of them every week. For example, I want to be able to get them ready for school in the mornings and to help them with their homework at night. I don't want to have them just on weekends.

Issue #3, Division of Your Marital Assets

Position-based statement: I want our family's Lexus SUV, not our Honda Civic.

Interest-based statement: As a realtor, I need a comfortable, roomy vehicle for my clients to ride in when I am showing them properties.

Joel and Cindy Curtis are getting a collaborative divorce. They are the parents of three children ranging in age from six to 14 and they own a large home in an expensive neighborhood. Today they are meeting with their divorce team to try to decide what to do about their home.

At the start of their discussion, Cindy makes it clear that she wants to keep the home. She says that she believes the couple's children will feel more secure if they can continue living there. Joel on the other hand is adamant about selling the home so the couple can use the sales proceeds to pay down their joint debts and put the remaining money toward down payments on smaller homes in their current neighborhood. Joel notes that his solution will also help make their children feel secure because they will be able to remain at the schools they now attend and to continue playing with their same neighborhood friends. He also points out that living close to one another will make it easier for Cindy and him to co-parent their children.

Joel and Cindy together with their collaborative divorce team decide that they need more information before they can make an informed decision about their home. Therefore, the financial professional asks the couple to meet with a real estate broker to find out what their home is likely to sell for and to learn the cost of smaller homes in their same neighborhood. The financial professional explains that the information will give them an idea of how much of their marital debt they will be able to pay off by selling their home and therefore, how much money they'll have for down payments on new homes.

When Joel and Cindy's collaborative divorce team meets again two weeks later they review the information that Joel and Cindy have pulled together. It's clear to everyone that if the couple sells their home they will have enough cash to do what Joel wants to do. Cindy is not swayed however. She continues to want to keep the home. The financial professional suggests that they take another look at Cindy's post-divorce budget and zero in on the amount of money that the couple currently spends each month on their mortgage, insurance, property taxes, utilities and maintenance. Once they do, it's obvious to everyone but Cindy that she cannot afford to keep the home and so the meeting ends without any agreement on what to do with it.

After the meeting the financial professional talks with the other members of the team about Cindy's continued desire to keep her family home. They all agree that he should prepare two sets of financial forecasts for Cindy to help ensure that she has a clear understanding of how keeping the house will affect her post-divorce finances. One set of forecasts will assume that Cindy keeps the home; the other will assume that Cindy and Joel sell it. Meanwhile, the mental health professional meets with Cindy to explore whether there are other ways that she could help her kids feel safe besides holding on to the home. After they talk for a while about the children and what feeling safe means, Cindy begins to realize that achieving the goal is less about where her children live and more about how she and Joel co-parent them after their divorce.

A couple of days later, Cindy meets with the financial professional.

He hopes to help Cindy become more realistic about her post-divorce finances and to talk more with her about the two solutions Cindy and Joel have identified. During their discussions it becomes clear to him that after spending time with the mental health professional, Cindy has become more receptive to the idea of selling her home. In fact, after reviewing the financial forecasts he prepared for Cindy to help illustrate how her solution and Joel's would affect her finances short-term and long-term, Cindy concludes that keeping the home would be a bad idea for her financially and that Joel's suggestion is the better option. She is comfortable with that solution because she knows that she and Joel will continue to live in their current neighborhood and that they are both totally committed to their children.

Everyone Plays By the Same Set of Rules

By signing the collaborative divorce Participation Agreement, you and your spouse and your respective attorneys all agree to play by the same set of rules during your divorce. For example, your attorneys agree to:

- Help you and your spouse identify your divorce interests.
- Empower you to make all of the decisions in your divorce.
- Ensure that you have all of the information you need to make the decisions.
- Help you brainstorm possible solutions to the issues in your divorce, understand the consequences of each solution, and choose the solutions that satisfy as many of your individual and shared interests as possible.
- Abide by the protocols of practice issued by the Collaborative Law Institute of Texas, Inc. You can read these protocols at http://www.collablawtexas.com.

The agreement also sets out:

- How you and your spouse will select any outside experts the two of you may agree to use and how you will share the cost of their fees. For example, you may agree to hire a realtor together, an appraiser to value your fine art collection, and so on.

- How you'll ensure that all written and oral communications related to your divorce will remain confidential.
- The rules you will follow when you and your spouse communicate with one another and with the members of your team.

An exhibit labeled *Code of Conduct* will be attached to your Participation Agreement. The Code of Conduct spells out specific actions that you and your spouse can and can't take during your divorce, most of which have the goal of preserving your marital assets. (Note: In a litigated divorce the court in most Texas jurisdictions attaches to the first pleading in the divorce -- usually the divorce petition -- a standing order with provisions that are very similar to what is in the Code of Conduct. So, regardless of whether you opt for a litigated or a collaborative divorce, there will be limitations on what you and your spouse can do with the money in your bank accounts while your divorce is going on, unless you and your spouse agree otherwise.)

Among other things, the Code of Conduct says that you cannot:

- Withdraw money from your checking or savings accounts for any reason unless you both agree to the withdrawal in writing or the reason is specified in your Participation Agreement. This does not mean however that you must have a specific agreement with your spouse in order to use the money in your bank accounts to pay your *reasonable and necessary* living and business expenses. Examples of *reasonable and necessary* living expenses include the cost of food, shelter, clothing, transportation, and childcare. In other words, while your divorce is going on the two of you can continue to operate pretty much as you always have financially. The goal of this provision is to prevent you and your spouse from spending the money in your bank accounts on out-of-the-ordinary expenses, like buying a motorcycle or going on a cruise, without the other's up-front okay.

- Damage any of your tangible property, like real estate, vehicles, boats, furniture, and fine art.
- Take on any new debt unless both of you agree to it in writing or it's specified in your Participation Agreement.
- Change the beneficiary designation on any of your insurance policies, retirement plans or pensions unless you and your spouse both agree to the change in writing.
- Destroy or alter any of your family's financial records.

There is a copy of the Code of Conduct in the appendix to this book. It's Exhibit A in the Participation Agreement.

During a collaborative divorce it's not unusual for a spouse to violate the terms of the Participation Agreement or the Code of Conduct in some way. More often than not, the violation is inadvertent. Here are two examples of unintentional violations and what the spouse who committed the violation should have done instead:

- You've always managed your family's investments. During your divorce in reaction to what is happening in the stock market you sell all of the stocks that you and your spouse own and put all of the cash from the sale in your joint money market account. Although you were looking out for the best interests of the two of you when you sold the stocks, you really should have told your spouse ahead of time that you wanted to sell them (and your team members too) and then completed the sale, assuming you both agreed that it was appropriate.
- During your divorce your spouse totals his car and purchases a new one without first telling you and the members of your team that he wants to buy the car. Furthermore, when he finances the purchase he puts the car loan in his name only. Although your spouse violated the terms of the Code of Conduct by doing so, the violation was not malicious or deliberate. In fact, he put the minimum down on the car in order to minimize the amount of money that would have to come out of your joint bank account. However, what your

spouse should have done was to tell you and your team members that his car had been totaled and ask for your okay to finance the purchase of a new car.

In some collaborative divorces however, one spouse may knowingly ignore the requirements of the Participation Agreement or Code of Conduct in order to try to cheat the other. Here's an example: *Diane Kimbrough is living in her family's home while she and her husband Jack are getting divorced. Diane knows that she is going to get the home in their divorce, so without letting Jack or their divorce team know, she pulls $100,000 out of one of the couple's joint bank accounts and uses the money to make improvements to the home. She is not upfront with Jack and her team members about her plans as she should have been because she knows that they would not have approved of them.*

If your spouse knowingly flaunts the requirements of the Participation Agreement or Code of Conduct, the members of your team will give her an opportunity to correct or undo what she did wrong. If your spouse balks at doing so, her attorney will remind your spouse that unless she corrects her error according to the terms of the Participation Agreement or Code of Conduct, your collaborative divorce will have to end, your attorneys will have to withdraw from your case, and you'll have to pursue a litigated divorce. Her attorney will also explain how the court would probably decide the issues in your divorce if it went to trial. (By the way, if you and your spouse were pursuing a litigated divorce and your spouse did what Diane Kimbrough did, or something equally inappropriate, the judge presiding over your divorce would not appreciate her behavior either and would have made her undo what she did or would have undone it for her.) If necessary, your spouse's attorney will also ask one or both of the two neutrals on your team to try to help persuade your spouse to comply with the Participation Agreement or Code of Conduct.

Tip: Talk to your attorney if you are not sure whether an action you want to take would violate the terms of your Participation Agreement or Code of Conduct. Also, if you are about to take an action that you are sure is okay, but you are concerned that your spouse may perceive it as a violation, it's a good idea to let your spouse know what you are about to do. (Keep your team members in the loop too.) Being up-front with your spouse will help minimize the likelihood that she'll misinterpret your action, which could complicate your divorce.

After ten years of marriage, Jim and Julie Patton are getting a collaborative divorce. Throughout their marriage Jim has handled all of their investments, including managing Julie's 401(k), because he knows a lot more about investing than Julie does.

After their divorce has begun, Jim sees some dark clouds on the economic horizon and decides that it would be a good idea to sell some of the stocks in Julie's 401(k). His goal is to minimize any potential losses and to put Julie in a good position to purchase new stocks at low prices when the time is right. Although he has carte blanche to manage her account, Jim decides to check with Julie anyway before he sells her stocks so that she understands what he wants to do and why.

Jim schedules a time to meet with Julie over coffee. During their meeting, he explains what he wants to do with her 401(k) and reviews the potential up and downsides of his plan. Julie listens intently to everything he says and when Jim is finished talking she tells him how much she appreciates his explaining everything to her. She also tells Jim that she wants him to do whatever he thinks is best for her financially.

Julie feels very good after the meeting is over. She is happy that Jim is obviously concerned about her financial welfare and appreciates that he took the time to talk to her about what he would like to do with her retirement account. Julie feels that Jim clearly demonstrated his respect for her and so she is confident that even though their marriage is ending he will continue to look out for her financial interests.

Julie's good feelings toward Jim are in evidence at their next team meeting when they revisit some issues that they'd not been able to resolve at their last meeting. It's much easier this time for the couple to work through those issues because Julie is no longer suspicious of every solution that Jim proposes. She feels a lot more confident about his intentions.

Your Kids Come First

In a litigated divorce, it's not unusual for parents to get so caught up in the process and to become so overwhelmed by their own emotions that they fail to protect their young children from their divorce and cause them emotional harm as a result. Some parents even involve their children in their divorce. For example, these parents may speak disparagingly about one another in front of their kids; ask their young children to choose sides in their divorce; have emotional meltdowns around them; turn their children into their divorce confidantes; grill them about who Mommy or Daddy went on a date with last night; use their kids as pawns in an effort to get the settlement agreement they want, and so on. Furthermore, these parents may continue victimizing their kids after their divorce is final by criticizing one another's parenting skills in front of them, turning their kids into go-betweens, fighting over them, and not living up to their child support obligations, among other things.

Warning! Studies show that children who are the victims of their parents' adversarial divorce often have emotional problems as adults.

Although there is no guarantee that your children won't have emotional problems if you get a collaborative divorce, there is less potential for problems with that kind of divorce compared to a litigated divorce because of two fundamental assumptions: Parents who pursue a collaborative divorce want to protect their children from their divorce and are willing to put their children's needs before their own. In order to help parents do so, the mental health professional will:

- Help prepare the two of you to tell your children about your divorce, if you have not already told them about your plans. She will even arm you with the right words to say when you're talking to your kids.
- Help you manage your emotions so that they won't get out of control and affect your kids.
- Provide you with information about the most common signs of emotional distress in children, and if your children begin having problems because of your divorce, she will advise

you about how to respond. For example, she may suggest that you spend more time with them, talk to them about what is bothering them, and/or set up a time for them to meet with a child therapist. The mental health professional may also meet with your children so that they can tell her what they are worried about, what they need from you to feel safe, and so that she can help them become comfortable talking with you and your spouse about your divorce. The mental health professional will also tell you what not to do if your children appear to be having emotional problems because of your divorce. As needed, the mental health professional can also help prepare your children to talk with their family members and friends about your divorce, including helping them anticipate the kinds of questions they may be asked and suggesting ways for them to respond.

Also, in order to make sure that you put your children's needs first during your divorce, you and your spouse will:

- Pledge to avoid inappropriate communications about your divorce with your children and agree to talk to them about your divorce only when the two of you agree that it's appropriate.
- Work with the mental health professional on the preparation of a detailed parenting plan that spells out your individual and joint rights and responsibilities as parents, among other things. The plan will become part of your final divorce decree. In preparation for writing this plan, the mental health professional may talk with your children about their schedules during the school week and on weekends and about their after-school activities, among other things. Chapter 5 of this book discusses parenting plans in detail.

There's No Formal Discovery

As you learned in the previous chapter, most litigated divorces involve a lot of formal discovery, which increases the cost of a divorce and makes the process more stressful. In a collaborative divorce there is no need for formal discovery because everyone involved agrees to freely share with one another all of the information you and your spouse need to negotiate the terms of your divorce. The two of you also agree to work together to obtain any missing information that you may need. For example, you and your spouse may agree to jointly hire a realtor to tell you what your home is worth and to have a business appraiser value your joint business. The team will help you identify and hire qualified appraisers such as these.

Creativity Is Encouraged

The issues in a litigated divorce are decided in light of what the law says, even if "what the law says" isn't in your best interest or in the best interest of your spouse or kids. But in a collaborative divorce, you're not constrained by the law; it is simply information that you may want to take into account during your negotiations, not the rule. Therefore you and your spouse can respond to the unique needs of your family by identifying creative, outside-the-box solutions to the issues in your divorce. For example, the Texas Family Code (the law) includes a standard possession schedule that the court is likely to award the non-primary parent in a litigated divorce. It states that the parent who does not have possession of the child on his birthday will have time with him from 6-8pm on that day. However, many families do not like this standard provision. In a collaborative divorce, couples are free to deal with birthdays however they want. For example, they may decide that whichever parent has the child on the date of the child's birthday gets to celebrate with the child and that the other parent celebrates with the child on a date close to the child's birthday; that they will celebrate the birthday as a family -- both parents and the child (or children) together; or that in odd years Mom will be with the child on his birthday from 5-9PM and in even years Dad will be with the child on that day.

You Always Know What's Going to Happen Next

Litigated divorces tend to be full of unexpected twists and turns because there is little if any cooperation between sides, the attorneys try not to signal their next moves to one another, and because both attorneys try to out-lawyer/out-maneuver the other in order to gain an advantage for their clients. As a result, going through a litigated divorce often feels like you've taken a ride on a very scary roller coaster.

In contrast, the collaborative divorce process is very predictable because everyone is working together toward the same goal and going to court isn't an option. Therefore, the attorneys have no reason to try to catch one another off guard or to put the other on the defensive. In addition, prior to each team meeting the attorneys, in consultation with the mental health and financial professionals, prepare a written meeting agenda and provide you and your spouse with a copy. As a result, you always know ahead of time exactly what you'll be discussing at your next meeting and you have time to prepare for those discussions with your attorney and the two neutrals. Being prepared for what's to come will help you feel less anxious and stressed out and make you more confident of your ability to make good decisions in your divorce. Furthermore, if you or your spouse tries to raise an issue in a joint meeting that isn't on the agenda for that particular meeting, you won't go ahead and discuss it anyway. Instead, the issue will be put on the agenda for a future meeting. Handling discussions about unscheduled issues this way means that one spouse can't take the other by surprise or put the other on the spot.

You Focus On the Future, Not On The Past

A collaborative divorce is fundamentally a future-oriented process. Therefore, you're less apt to make short-sighted decisions that might satisfy your needs next month, next year or the year after for example, but would not be in your long term best interest.

Focusing on the future also helps minimize the likelihood that you'll try to use your divorce to relive all of the things that went wrong in your marriage or to punish your spouse for what you believe he did to contribute to the end of your marriage, things that often happen in litigated divorces. If you do, the members of your team will help you regain your focus.

Also, because of the forward focus of the collaborative process, no one on your divorce team will accuse you of being a lousy spouse or bring up all of your shortcomings. In a litigated divorce however, your spouse's attorney is apt to do just that in order to put your spouse in a better position.

You're Helped to Feel Safe

One of the goals of the collaborative divorce process is to help you feel safe during your divorce, something that you probably won't feel in a litigated divorce given the unpredictability and adversarial nature of the process. If you feel safe, it will be easier for you to fully participate in the collaborative process and to be an effective advocate for yourself because:

- You'll feel free to express your interests and concerns.
- You won't be afraid that you'll pay a price if you let your guard down and are emotionally vulnerable in front of your spouse and the team.
- You won't feel pressured to accept a settlement agreement that you don't like or to make a decision by a certain deadline.
- Your spouse and his attorney won't try to intimidate you.
- Your needs and opinions will be respected and you'll be heard by your spouse and the members of your divorce team.
- No one will threaten to take you to court.

Feeling safe during the collaborative divorce process however does not mean that you'll never feel upset or ill at ease because of something your spouse may say, information you may have to share with your spouse and your divorce team, decisions you have to make during your divorce, and so on. After all, you will be dealing with difficult issues during your team meetings and so you are bound to feel uncomfortable sometimes. Even so, the collaborative process will make it easier for you to bring up subjects you feel awkward about, honestly express your opinions, and so on.

You Get Help Handling Your Emotions

Going through a divorce is an intense emotional experience for nearly everyone no matter what the process. However, one of the benefits of a collaborative divorce is that your team members will help you manage your emotions so that they are less apt to interfere with your ability to make good decisions and make your divorce more difficult. For example, if the mental health professional notices during a team meeting that things are getting tense between you and your spouse or that one or both of you is having a difficult time staying focused on the agenda item you are supposed to be discussing, the mental health professional may:

-- Suggest that you and your spouse agree to take a short break from your negotiations so that you can have some time to calm down, maybe by taking a walk.
-- Talk with you and your attorney about what's bothering you and explain why you need to "get your act together".
-- Suggest that the two of you meet one-on-one so she can understand why you are so upset and suggest things you can do to manage your emotions.
-- Refer you to a mental health therapist, if she believes that you would benefit from some on-going therapy. As a neutral member of your team, the mental health professional cannot act as your therapist.
-- Recommend that you and your spouse consider suspending your negotiations for a while if you are too emotional to be a productive participant in your divorce.

In a litigated divorce, there will be no mental health professional monitoring how well you are coping with your divorce as you go through the process and providing you with support when you need it.

Many couples find that because they receive help handling their emotions within the structure of the collaborative divorce process, it's a lot easier for them to be pleasant to one another outside of their team meetings. This is a particularly important benefit of a collaborative divorce if they are raising young children together.

Your Family's Privacy is Protected

The details of your marriage -- your financial situation, the nature of the problems between you and your spouse, your own problems, and anything else related to your divorce that you would prefer to keep private -- stay private in a collaborative divorce because it's a non-court process. Only you and your spouse and the members of your divorce team will know them.

In a litigated divorce, the details of your divorce will be in the public record and available to anyone who wants to go to the courthouse and read them, like your nosy neighbors and relatives perhaps, unless you and/or your spouse ask the court to seal your file. Furthermore anyone who wants to can attend the hearings in your divorce and your divorce trial too, if there is one.

All of the Money You Spend Goes Toward a Settlement

Getting divorced is almost never an inexpensive proposition. However, your money will be better spent in a collaborative divorce because going to court is off the table so every penny you and your spouse spend on your divorce -- your attorney's fees and expenses, your share of the cost of the mental health and financial professionals on your team and of any outside specialists you may hire -- goes toward helping you negotiate a settlement.

In contrast, the cost of a litigated divorce will include not just the amount of money it costs for your attorney to try to negotiate your settlement agreement, but also the amount it costs for your attorney to prepare for the possibility that your divorce will go to trial. Given that most litigated divorces are eventually settled outside of court, you'll probably pay for services that you'll never need.

Co-Parenting Your Kids is Easier

It's a basic tenet of the collaborative divorce process: Children of divorce do best when their parents raise them together (even though the parents are no longer married and living together) and when their sense of family (albeit a restructured family) is preserved.

The process makes it easier for you and your spouse to do both by helping you:

- Improve your abilities to communicate with one another and resolve problems together.
- Accept your differences as parents.
- Prepare a detailed written parenting plan, which will be your post-divorce parenting roadmap. Parenting plans are discussed in Chapter 5.
- Understand that although your divorce ends your marriage, it does not have to end your family too. The mental health professional will explain that you can still be a family after your divorce, just a different kind of family -- one with two parents living in different homes. Thinking of yourselves as a redefined family will make it easier for the two of you to work together to give your children what they need from you now and in the years to come.

You Get Help Healing

Can a divorce help you heal from the pain of your failed marriage? Yes, if it's a collaborative divorce. Although getting divorced is almost always an emotionally difficult experience regardless of how you do it, the collaborative process makes it easier to begin healing from the pain. This is because during your divorce the members of your team will help you:

- Understand and manage your emotions rather than having them control you.
- Accept what has happened to your marriage and the changes that are occurring in your life as a result.
- Focus on the future rather than staying stuck in the past.
- Possibly forgive your spouse for whatever he may have done to end your marriage and forgive yourself if you are wracked with guilt over things you did (or didn't do) that you believe contributed to its failure.

If you and your spouse opt for a litigated divorce, there will be no divorce team by your side to help you manage your emotions, put your failed marriage in perspective, and begin moving your life forward.

There is Less Potential for Problems With Your Spouse After Your Divorce

In a collaborative divorce, no one will tell you how to resolve the issues in your divorce, no one will pressure you to agree to terms that you don't like, and no judge or jury will decide those terms for you. You and your spouse will decide everything. Compared to a litigated divorce therefore, it's much less likely that there will be any conflict between you and your spouse over the terms of your divorce once you're no longer husband and wife.

Figure 2.2, Top Eight Questions Spouses Ask About the Collaborative Divorce Process

Spouses who are considering getting a collaborative divorce usually have a lot of questions about how the process works and they often have mistaken impressions of the process too. This section of the chapter features some of their most frequently asked questions and provides an answer for each one.

I heard that if the collaborative divorce process doesn't work and my spouse and I go to court, we'll have to fire our lawyers and get new ones. Is this true?

Yes, if you decide to end the collaborative process you and your spouse must fire your lawyers and hire new ones. In most collaborative divorces, this fact gives the lawyers and the spouses a big incentive to be creative in their problem solving and to stick with the process so that they can reach an agreement that is acceptable to both spouses. Too often in litigated divorces, when one of the lawyers or one of the spouses is feeling angry, their knee jerk reaction is to say, "Fine, I'll see you in court". That is much less likely to happen in a collaborative divorce.

Is it true that in a collaborative divorce, attorneys just give in to the other side rather than fighting to ensure that their clients get a good deal?

No, that is not true. Your lawyer is still your advocate and works hard to get you a good deal. Your lawyer still "fights" for you, but it's not the kind of fighting that happens in too many litigated divorces. Your collaborative divorce attorney will "fight" for you by working hard during the divorce process to come up with creative solutions to the issues in your divorce that meet the needs of you and your spouse (and your young children) and that are acceptable to you both.

Does collaborative law lend itself to delays? Could a spouse use it to delay getting a divorce?

If you or your spouse want to delay, you could do so in both a collaborative divorce and a traditional litigated divorce. Delays are not unique to the collaborative process. However, in a collaborative divorce, your team will try to minimize the potential for delays by establishing a timeline that everyone will agree to work towards. If you or your spouse refuses to move forward despite your team's best efforts to meet that timeline, your attorneys would opt out of the collaborative process so that your divorce could be set for trial. However, this does not happen very often in collaborative divorce.

Is the collaborative approach a good idea if you don't trust your spouse at all? What if you think he has hidden assets?

It is very common for spouses not to trust one another at the beginning of a divorce case. Lack of trust is often what caused their divorce in the first place. Even so, the collaborative divorce process can be very successful. If you have concerns about assets you think your spouse may be hiding, it is particularly helpful to have a neutral financial planner involved in your divorce, as would be the case if you pursued a collaborative divorce.

Why do my spouse and I need a mental health professional involved in our collaborative divorce? We already tried marital counseling and it didn't work.

The mental health professional will not act as your therapist/counselor in your collaborative divorce. Instead of focusing on the problems in your marriage, the mental health professional will support and facilitate productive communication between you and your spouse and among the members of your team and will help ensure that the collaborative process works effectively. The mental health professional will help keep everyone focused on the issues at hand during your team meetings and will help everyone manage their emotions so that they don't derail your efforts to find solutions to each of the issues in your divorce and so that you and your spouse can end up with a divorce settlement agreement that is acceptable to both of you.

I have a lot of concerns about how my divorce will affect the amount of time I have with my children and my relationship with them. Will I end up being just a weekend parent? Given that my children are very young, will my divorce affect my ability to have them stay with me overnight? What about their after-school activities -- are they likely to affect their time with me?

In a collaborative divorce, you and your spouse will talk with the members of your team about your goals and interests regarding your young children and about your parenting time with them. (By the way, in a collaborative divorce terms like "visitation" and "visitation schedule" are not used. The phrase "parenting time" is used instead.) Once the team understands your goals, you and your spouse will meet with the mental health professional apart from the other team members to develop a written parenting plan that works for you and your children. Among other things, you and your spouse will discuss how you want to handle your parenting time week-to-week, during the summers, on holidays, birthdays, and so on in light of what is best for your children and their individual needs. In a collaborative divorce you as parents, not a judge, develop your parenting plan.

Can I get a better financial deal through a collaborative divorce?

Getting" a better deal" compared to a litigated divorce is *not* a reason to get a collaborative divorce. The reasons include to stay out of the court, to keep the details of your divorce private, and to have the freedom to structure a divorce agreement that works best for you, your spouse and your young children. Although you may ultimately end up with more income or assets through the collaborative process than you would have if you had pursued a litigated divorce, that outcome is not a given simply because of the collaborative divorce process.

Will the financial professional on my collaborative divorce team give my spouse and me advice about how to divide up our assets and our liabilities?

The financial professional will not give you any financial advice or tell you whether a financial solution you are considering is good or bad. Your attorney is the only person on your divorce team who will give you advice. The role of the financial professional is to help facilitate the financial decisions you and your spouse will make during your divorce negotiations and to help the two of you understand the implications of a particular solution using financial projections, tax calculations and other tools.

Deciding if a Collaborative Divorce is Right For You

Although this chapter has highlighted the many attractive features and benefits associated with a collaborative divorce, the process is not for everyone. The following checklist, which represents the keys to a successful collaborative divorce, can help you decide if it's right for you. The more statements you answer "yes" to, the more suited you are to a collaborative divorce.

√ I am willing to take responsibility for the outcome of my

divorce and to fully commit to the process, even if I don't want my marriage to end.

√ I want to keep the courts out of my life and my family's life.

√ I am willing to do the hard work of negotiating a settlement agreement with my spouse.

√ I want to protect my children from any emotional trauma associated with my divorce.

√ During my divorce negotiations, I am willing to treat my spouse with respect and I want my spouse to treat me with respect too.

√ I will focus on my future during my divorce instead of using it to rehash the problems in my marriage or to punish my spouse for the things I think he did to ruin our relationship.

√ I want the details of my divorce kept private.

√ I want to have a respectful relationship with my spouse after our marriage has ended.

√ I am willing to seek treatment for my addiction or my mental health problem before I begin the collaborative divorce process, if needed.

Warning! If you are too fearful to sit in a room with your spouse and discuss your divorce needs and interests, maybe because your spouse has been abusive to you in the past and you are afraid that if you speak your mind he may harm you (or your children) again, the two of you won't be able to negotiate with one another as equals. As a result, a collaborative divorce is not for you.

Chapter #3, Going Through a Collaborative Divorce

This chapter offers a general overview of how your collaborative divorce will work. It begins with hiring an attorney and ends with your divorce becoming official. However, no collaborative divorce is exactly the same, so the actual events in yours will probably be a little different from what's described here.

Finding a Collaborative Divorce Attorney

If you decide to end your marriage through a collaborative divorce, you should hire a divorce attorney who has been trained in that process. The best way to do that is to develop a list of collaborative divorce attorneys (Four or five names is probably plenty.), meet with each of them, and then choose the attorney you think will do the best job for you. Here are some good ways to find attorneys to put on your list:

- Visit the web site of the Collaborative Law Institute of Texas (CLI-TX) www.collablawtexas.com. You can search for divorce attorneys in your particular part of the state at this site.
- Ask any friends, relatives or co-workers you may know who got a collaborative divorce for the names of their attorneys, assuming they were happy with the legal help they received.
- Contact your local or state bar association for referrals to some collaborative divorce attorneys in your area.

Once you have a list of attorneys, schedule an initial consultation, or meeting, with each one. The consultations will give you an opportunity to find out how each attorney would approach your divorce, whether any of the attorneys have ever handled a divorce like yours, assuming there is something unique or complex about it -- you and your spouse share a business or you have a substantial amount of wealth, for example -- the number of collaborative divorces each of the attorneys has handled (the more the better), their fees, and how much your legal expenses are likely to be. The attorneys will also use the meetings to learn some initial information about you. For example, they will probably want to find out a little about your marriage, the reason for your divorce, how much you know about the collaborative divorce process, and why you want to use a collaborative rather than a litigated divorce to end your marriage. Tip: Generally, the more collaborative divorces an attorney has handled the more skilled the attorney will be at guiding you through the process, making effective use of the neutral professionals on your divorce team, and helping you and your spouse reach a negotiated settlement.

At your attorney meetings, take note of how comfortable you feel with each attorney, how good a job an attorney does at answering your questions in plain English, and whether any of the attorneys seem more or less interested in your divorce. These observations combined with the information you learn about each attorney's collaborative divorce experience will help you choose the best attorney for you.

After You've Hired an Attorney

Once you've hired an attorney, the two of you will meet so that the attorney can learn more about you, your spouse and your marriage. For example, your attorney will try to get a sense of where you are in the divorce grieving process and of your attitudes toward your spouse and your divorce, your emotional hot buttons, and the kinds of help you may need from the mental health and financial professionals. Your attorney will also discuss the philosophy and goals of the collaborative process, introduce you to the concept of interest-based negotiating, explain your role in the process and what will be expected of you, and will ask if there are any issues in your divorce that you want resolved as soon as possible on a temporary basis. For example, you may want to decide right away how your marital bills will be paid during your divorce, how you and your spouse will handle the support and parenting of your young children, which of you can remain in your home while your divorce is going on, whether you'll receive temporary spousal support, and so on. Your attorney will make sure that such issues are on the agenda for your first team meeting.

Tip: Be honest and forthcoming with your attorney about your marriage even if some of the details are embarrassing. Your information will help your attorney figure out how to manage your divorce, anticipate potential obstacles to a resolution of the issues in your divorce, and identify the kinds of help you may need in order to overcome those issues, among other things.

You'll be able to ask your attorney questions during the meeting. For example, if your spouse has not already agreed to a collaborative divorce, you may want advice about the best way to broach the subject with him. Figure 3.1 offers some tips.

After the meeting your attorney's paralegal will send you:

- A copy of the Participation Agreement. For a discussion of this agreement, turn back to Chapter 2.
- Copies of the contracts used by the mental health and financial professionals who will be on your divorce team. Their contracts will be very similar to the Participation Agreement.
- A divorce goals worksheet for you to complete. (You'll find a sample goals worksheet in the appendix to this book.) Among other things, the worksheet asks you to:

    -- Define the goals you have for your divorce and clarify why each goal is important to you. Your particular goals will depend on your values, your financial situation, whether or not you and your spouse have young children together, the life you envision for yourself post-divorce, and so on.

    -- Write down what you think your spouse's goals are and why you think they are important to him. As you complete this exercise you may realize that the two of you have some goals in common.

    -- List the things that scare or worry you most about getting divorced and about the collaborative process in particular. For example, you may be afraid that after your divorce you won't have enough money to live on and/or that you won't be able to spend as much time with your children as you do now; you may be concerned that you won't be an effective advocate for your own interests during your divorce negotiations; and/or you may be worried about the idea of sitting down at the same table as your spouse.

-- List what you think your spouse is most worried or scared about.

-- Describe the goals you have for your children. You may want them to continue taking private music lessons, going to Summer camp and having the opportunity to spend quality time with you and your spouse each week, for example.

-- Describe the kind of relationship you'd like to have with your spouse once your marriage ends. You may want to be friends with her, to have a cordial relationship with one another because of your kids, or you may not want anything to do with your spouse once your marriage is over.

-- Identify what would most concern you about the litigated divorce process should the collaborative process not work for you and your spouse. For example, you may be afraid that your spouse will hire a better attorney than you can afford since he makes a lot more money than you do, or that you will not get custody of your children.

Completing the goals worksheet may make it easier for you to begin to "put yourself in your spouse's shoes." If you can do that, it will be easier for you to respect your spouse's interests during your negotiations and to work with your spouse to find solutions to the issues in your divorce that satisfy those interests as well as your own.

Figure 3.1, Talking to Your Spouse About a Collaborative Divorce

If you want a collaborative divorce, but you don't know if your spouse does, you'll have to broach the subject with him. Before you do, you should spend some time thinking about exactly how to go about it because the approach you use could make the difference between your spouse agreeing to a collaborative divorce and refusing to even consider one. Your options include:

- Have a face-to-face conversation with your spouse. This is your best option if the two of you still have a civil relationship with one another and you feel that you can calmly and clearly articulate why a collaborative divorce would be better for the two of you (and for your young children) than a litigated divorce.
- Write your spouse a letter. Putting your thoughts on paper is a good option if you and your spouse aren't talking to one another, your conversations with one another always end badly, or if you usually express your thoughts best in writing.
- Ask someone your spouse trusts and respects to talk with him about ending your marriage with a collaborative divorce. He may be more receptive to the idea if it comes from someone other than you, especially if your spouse doesn't want your marriage to end. However, before you ask someone else to talk with your spouse, try to confirm that your spouse has already told that person that you are divorcing. If your spouse has not, he may become very upset that you, not him, told that person that your marriage is ending, and your spouse may refuse to even consider a collaborative divorce as a result.
- Ask your divorce attorney to write your spouse a letter informing him that you want to end your marriage through a collaborative divorce and explaining why that kind of divorce will be better for your spouse than a litigated divorce.

Regardless of how you broach the subject of a collaborative divorce, it's a good idea to provide your spouse with a written overview of how it will work, an explanation of its advantages, and if you have young children, an explanation of why the process would be best for them. Give your spouse a list of collaborative divorce attorneys in your area as well. Your attorney should be able to provide you with all of this information.

If your spouse refuses to consider a collaborative divorce, don't push the matter. Give him some time to think about your suggestion and then bring it up again. If you wait a while, you may find that he's had a change of heart.

Tip: You may need to swallow your pride and accept responsibility for your part in the failure of your marriage if you want your spouse to agree to a collaborative divorce. Another option is to ask your spouse to try the collaborative process with the understanding that if she doesn't like it you'll agree to pursue a litigated divorce instead. There is a good chance that if your spouse goes along with your suggestion and maintains an open mind, she'll stick with the process.

Stephanie Mathews is devastated. She thought she and her husband Will had the perfect marriage. After all, they are both successful professionals, make plenty of money, have a nice home and lots of friends. However, she learned recently that Will was having an affair and after Stephanie confronted him about it, the couple decided to end their 20-year marriage.

After talking over their options, Stephanie and Will decide to get a collaborative divorce. They like the fact that the process will be private and will make it easier for them to avoid a messy divorce.

At their first team meeting, it becomes obvious that although Will is anxious to put his marriage behind him as quickly as possible, Stephanie is having a hard time accepting the idea of divorce and is very angry with Will. After the meeting is over, their attorneys and the two neutrals discuss the situation during a conference call. They all agree that unless Stephanie can get a handle on her emotions and gain some perspective on why her marriage has failed, she'll have a difficult time working out the terms of her divorce with Will and the collaborative process may not work for them. Therefore, the attorneys and the two neutrals all agree that they should suggest to the couple that they put their divorce on hold for a couple months so that Stephanie can work with a therapist.

Stephanie's attorney and the mental health professional meet with Stephanie to let her know about the team's recommendation. At first Stephanie denies that she is too emotionally distraught to participate in the collaborative divorce process, but after the three of them spend some time talking, she concedes that their suggestion is a good one. The mental health professional gives Stephanie the names of a couple therapists.

Next, the mental health professional meets with Will and his attorney to discuss delaying the divorce while Stephanie works with a therapist. Reluctantly, Will agrees to a delay.

When Stephanie and Will resume their divorce, it's obvious that Stephanie is in a better place. Her therapy helped her accept the fact that her marriage is over and understand that Will's affair was a symptom of problems in their marriage that neither one of them had been willing to acknowledge, not the cause of their divorce. She is also much less angry with Will (although she is still hurt by the fact that he has been having an affair). As a result, the couple is able to complete their collaborative divorce relatively easily. In the end, Stephanie and Will feel good about how they ended their marriage, especially because the process made it possible for them to honor the good aspects of their relationship and remain friends. In fact, after signing their divorce decree in the office of Will's attorney, they spend time alone in that room crying and hugging one another.

The Team Meetings in Your Divorce

You and your spouse will work out the terms of your divorce during a series of team meetings, each of which will probably last about two hours and be spaced about two weeks apart. If your collaborative divorce is like most others, it will take you and your spouse somewhere between three and six meetings to resolve all of the issues in your divorce. Exactly how many meetings it takes will depend on the complexity of the issues in your divorce and on how well you and your spouse are able to work together, among other things.

The location for each of your team meetings will probably alternate between your attorney's office and the office of your spouse's attorney, or the neutral professionals' offices. However, the two of you can agree to a different arrangement if you want.

The team meetings are where the hard work of your divorce gets done. Your attorney and the two neutrals will prepare you for each of the meetings and will actively participate in them. They will also prepare themselves for each meeting during a conference call. Among other things, they will discuss the issues you and your spouse will be negotiating, any problems they anticipate and how to handle them, and any new information they may have learned that is relevant to your divorce, among other things.

After each conference call the attorneys will prepare a written agenda for the upcoming meeting. You and your spouse will receive copies. Also, after each meeting is over, you'll each receive a set of written minutes that detail the decisions you may have reached during the meeting, any homework you may have been asked to complete, and so on.

Tip: Let your attorney know right away if anything in your life changes during your divorce. For example, you lose your job or get a salary increase, you and your spouse receive a foreclosure notice from the company that is holding your home mortgage, your teenage son begins treatment for depression, your spouse mentions suicide, and so on. The two attorneys and the two neutrals will decide how to respond to the change.

Getting Ready For Your First Team Meeting

You and your attorney will meet with one another at least once to prepare for your first team meeting. As part of the preparations your attorney will:

- Ask you questions to get a sense of how well you are coping emotionally.
- Find out if any new issues have developed in your divorce since the last time you talked.
- Explain what will happen at the meeting.
- Remind you about what is expected of you during your divorce and how you can contribute to the success of the collaborative process -- avoid losing control of your emotions, be honest and transparent, respect your spouse, and so on.

- Review the information on your goals worksheet. The attorney may ask you to clarify some of the goals and to prioritize your goals so that you are clear about which ones are most and least important to you. She may also suggest other goals you may want to consider. If your attorney thinks that any of your goals are unrealistic, she will try to help you develop a better sense of what's possible and likely in your divorce.
- Ask you again if there are any issues that you want resolved temporarily.
- Answer any questions you may have about your first team meeting and about the collaborative divorce process in general, and try to alleviate your concerns.

Your attorney will also let you know that she will begin trying to establish a good rapport with your spouse at your initial team meeting and that your spouse's attorney will try to do the same with you. She'll explain why it's important that you and your spouse have a positive, trusting relationship with both attorneys and she'll reassure you that her friendliness with your spouse will in no way compromise her commitment to protecting your interests. *You* will be her number one concern. Your attorney will also let you know that your spouse's attorney, the two neutrals and your spouse may ask you questions during your team meetings and that you can ask them questions too. She'll explain that because the collaborative divorce process is non-adversarial you won't have to worry about whether any of your answers will be used against you later and whether anyone will be trying to get you to say something that might be damaging to you.

At the First Team Meeting

Your first team meeting will lay the groundwork and set a tone for the rest of your meetings. At the meeting's end, assuming everything went well, you will probably feel a little more comfortable with the collaborative process and more ready to move forward.

Although no initial team meeting is exactly the same, here is a general rundown of what will probably happen at yours:

- You'll meet your spouse's attorney for the first time and the two of you will begin getting to know one another. Your attorney and your spouse will do the same.
- The attorneys will review the Participation Agreement with you and your spouse one more time and answer any questions you may have about it. Then the four of you will sign the agreement, which will mark the official start of the collaborative divorce process.
- The mental health and financial professionals will introduce themselves and explain their roles in your divorce. They will also go over their own agreements with you, answer any questions you may have and then you and your spouse and the two neutrals will sign the agreements.
- You and your spouse may be asked to explain why you've chosen a collaborative divorce.
- You and your spouse will talk about your goals and interests so that you each understand what the other needs from your divorce and so that you are both aware of any goals and interests you may have in common.
- Everyone will discuss the main issues in your divorce and identify the information you'll need to resolve them. You'll also decide how you'll obtain any information you don't already have. Figure 3.2 provides a list of the kinds of financial information you'll be asked to pull together.
- You and your spouse will discuss the issues you want settled temporarily and if you have time, you'll try to resolve each of them at the first meeting. If you don't have time, you'll take them up at your next team meeting. Before that meeting you may meet with one or both of the neutral professionals to discuss possible solutions to those issues so that you'll have less to negotiate at the meeting.

Tip. No matter how well prepared you are for your first team meeting, you'll probably feel nervous going into it. That's no surprise given that you're beginning a very important process in your life and that you'll be sharing personal, maybe even embarrassing information about yourself and your marriage with four people you hardly know.

On top of all that, during the meeting you and your spouse will be sitting at the same table, which may be very difficult for you if you have not spoken with one another for months much less been in the same room. To help calm your nerves, get a good sleep the night before the meeting and try to do something that relaxes you -- go for a run, take a hot bath, read a good book, or do yoga, for example.

Tip: There will be a lot of paperwork to review at your first meeting and the members of your team will also spend time reviewing the collaborative divorce process with you and your spouse. Therefore, it will probably seem like the meeting lasts a long time. Be patient however, because the first meeting lays the groundwork for an effective collaborative divorce process.

Warning! If someone on your divorce team asks you to do some homework on your own, it's important to the integrity of the collaborative divorce process that you complete it and that you complete it on time. If you don't, not only will you slow down your divorce, but you may also jeopardize the process should your spouse begin to doubt your commitment to it and start questioning as a result whether she'd be better off getting a litigated divorce.

Before the end of your first team meeting, everyone will agree on a date, time and place for the next one and anything that you didn't discuss will be moved to the agenda for that meeting. Also, the two neutrals will schedule times to meet with you and your spouse individually and together so that they can get to know you better and begin working with you on some of the issues in your divorce. The more you can accomplish between your team meetings, the smoother those meetings will go and the sooner your divorce will be over. For example, you and your spouse and the financial professional may meet to:

- Discuss how you and your spouse will divide up your furniture and household goods.
- Talk about temporary resolutions to the financial issues in your divorce, assuming those issues were not resolved at the first team meeting.
- Review your post-divorce budgets.

And you may meet with the mental health professional to:

- Talk about how you'll tell your children about your divorce.
- Work on your communications skills.
- Begin preparing your parenting plan, if you and your spouse have minor children. Chapter 5 discusses parenting plans.

Sometime after your first team meeting, you and your attorney will talk about what happened at that meeting. (You'll do the same thing after each team meeting.) Let your attorney know if you are confused by anything or have any questions. The two of you may also review what you need to accomplish before your next team meeting. Meanwhile, your attorney, your spouse's attorney and the two neutrals will also go over what happened at the meeting, talk about how to handle any problems that may have surfaced, and decide what to put on the agenda for your next team meeting. They'll have a similar conversation after each team meeting in your divorce.

Figure 3.2, Your Financial Information

Everyone on your collaborative divorce team must have a complete picture of your family's finances in order to help you and your spouse negotiate the terms of your divorce. You and your spouse will be expected to provide most of the financial documents and other information they will need, although the financial professional will help you as necessary. The information you will be asked to provide includes:

- Your recent paycheck stubs or proof of the amount of money that your employer deposits directly into your bank account each pay period.
- Your most recent checking and savings account statements -- individual and joint.
- Your most recent statements for the individual and joint investments you own, including stocks, bonds, mutual funds, annuities, 401(k)s, Individual Retirement Accounts (IRAs), and limited partnerships. The financial professional will need

the same information for any Certificate of Deposits (CDs) you and/or your spouse own and for any employer-sponsored stock option plans, deferred compensation plans, or pensions you may be participating in.

- A copy of your life insurance policy/ies.
- A copy of any disability and long-term care insurance policies you may own.
- Your most recent tax returns.
- A copy of the last Schedule C you filed with the IRS, if you and/or your spouse are business owners.
- Your most recent mortgage statements for the real estate you and your spouse may own individually or together, including your personal residence, vacation home, rental property, commercial property, and so on. If you have had any of these properties appraised recently, provide copies of those appraisals.
- Information about any timeshares you have an interest in.
- A list of all of the vehicles you own, including their makes and models, years of manufacture, VINs (Vehicle Information Numbers), and *Kelly Blue Book* values. You can obtain a *Blue Book* value for each vehicle by going to www.kbb.com or by visiting your local library and consulting its copy of the *Kelly Blue Book*.
- A list of any motorcycles, recreational vehicles, watercraft and trailers you and your spouse may own.
- A copy of your most recent Social Security statements, if either of you is receiving Social Security payments.
- The most recent statement for each of your individual and joint outstanding debts, including your credit card debts, your mortgage, home equity loan, car loan, student loan, and so on.

The financial professional will also ask you and your spouse to fill out an *Inventory and Appraisement* form, which involves listing each of your marital debts and their outstanding balances and all of your significant assets, including your real estate, vehicles, retirement and investment accounts (but not miscellaneous assets like your household furniture, bedding, kitchen equipment, and so on) and their current values. If you don't know the value of a certain asset or if you and your spouse disagree about its value, the financial professional will try to help you resolve your differences or may suggest that you hire an appraiser to tell you what the asset is worth.

Negotiating the Terms of Your Divorce

Once you've gotten all of the preliminaries out of the way, you and your spouse will begin negotiating the terms of your divorce. Each time you tackle a specific issue, your goal will be to find a solution that satisfies as many of the interests you and your spouse have identified as possible. Most likely your team will have you start with an issue that they think will be relatively easy for you to resolve. An early negotiating success will help you and your spouse become more comfortable with the collaborative process and more confident in your ability to negotiate other issues together.

In general, the negotiating process will work like this:

- You and your spouse together with your team members will brainstorm possible solutions for the particular issue you're trying to resolve.

Tip. Don't automatically dismiss a possible solution because you think it's silly, impractical, too difficult, or too expensive. Considering the solution may help you come up with another more workable solution that would never have occurred to you otherwise.

- After you and your spouse feel that you've identified all possible solutions for the issue, the two of you with the help of your team, will begin evaluating each solution, eliminating the ones that you and your spouse don't like, that don't do a good job of satisfying the interests you've identified, and so on. Once you've narrowed down your list, you'll take a closer look at the remaining solutions and you'll try to reach an agreement with one another regarding which one is best. (The solution you decide on may actually be a combination of solutions.) As you go through the elimination process, your team members will make sure that you and your spouse thoroughly consider all aspects of each solution and understand each solution's practical implications. Also, the attorneys will let you know if a particular solution is going to be legally unenforceable. However, in a collaborative divorce you and your spouse can choose that solution anyway if it's the one you like best.

Sue and Alan Rothman are brainstorming what to do with their family home. With the help of their team they come up with five possible solutions:

1. *Sue will keep the home in exchange for taking over the mortgage payments and for paying Alan his share of the couple's equity in the home.*
2. *Alan will keep the home in exchange for taking over the mortgage payments and paying Sue her share of the equity.*
3. *Sue and Alan will continue to own the home together and will take turns living there; their minor children will live in the house full time. The couple will share the costs of their mortgage, taxes and insurance, and will also share any home repair and maintenance expenses according to a formula that the financial professional will develop for them based on their individual incomes.*
4. *Sue and Alan will rent out their home and will use the rental income to help pay their mortgage, taxes and insurance, and to help defray any home repair and maintenance expenses. The financial professional will help the couple figure out how to share any costs that the rental income may not cover as well as any profit they may realize from the rental of their home.*
5. *The couple will sell their home as soon as possible and split the net proceeds.*
6. *Sue and Alan will sell their home in two years and split the net proceeds. While they still own it together, whichever spouse is living in the home will be fully responsible for the monthly costs of living there. The financial professional will help them*

work out a formula for sharing other costs associated with their home, like property taxes.

About a week after the meeting is over, Sue and Alan meet with the financial professional to talk in detail about the financial implications of each of the solutions they've identified. They evaluate them in light of their post-divorce budgets and the long-term financial projections the financial professional has prepared for them. They also discuss how each solution would work practically. Both of them leave the meeting feeling a lot clearer about the solutions they've identified.

At their next team meeting Sue and Alan begin eliminating solutions. They eliminate solution #3 immediately because they know that neither of them will be able to afford to maintain two residences after their divorce and because they both agree that having their parents constantly moving from one residence to the other will be disruptive for their kids; Sue and Alan also agree that the arrangement will be stressful for both of them. Next they eliminate solution #4 because they've never owned rental property together before and don't think that the time to start is after they are divorced. They see too many potential pitfalls in such an arrangement and worry that if they clash as landlords their differences might make it more difficult for them to be good co-parents to their kids. After taking hard looks at their post-divorce budgets, Alan and Sue also cross solutions #1 and #2 off of their list because they've decided that they need to live in smaller homes that will cost them less to maintain. That leaves Sue and Alan with solutions #5 and #6. In the end, they choose solution #6 because although long term neither of them can afford the house, they both agree that it would be better for their family if they did not have to go through a divorce and move in the same year and that it will be best for their children if they put off selling and moving for two years.

If You and Your Spouse Get Stuck on an Issue

Although it may be fairly easy for you and your spouse to resolve some of the issues in your divorce, resolving others may be a challenge, maybe because they are very complex, they trigger a lot of emotion in one or both of you, or because you and your spouse have problems coming up with solutions for those issues that you both like, for example. To help you reach a decision on such issues, the members of your team may:

- Provide you with additional information and analysis.
- Tell you how other couples have resolved the same issues.
- Put new solutions on the table and encourage you to come up with new ones too.
- Suggest that you reconsider solutions you may have eliminated, maybe giving you new ways of thinking about them.
- Recommend that you and your spouse spend more time working on the issues with one or both of the two neutrals.

If you and your spouse remain deadlocked on an issue despite the help of your team, your attorneys will remind you that if the two of you can't reach an agreement with one another, the collaborative process will end, they will remove themselves from your case, and a judge or jury will have to resolve the issue for you. They'll also give you a reality check by telling you how the court would probably rule on the issue you are having problems resolving. In addition, your attorneys may suggest that you hire a mediator to try to help you end your stalemate.

If You Reach an Agreement On Everything

Once you and your spouse have resolved all of the issues in your divorce, your attorneys will draft a written settlement agreement that incorporates each of your decisions. This document is called an *Agreed Decree of Divorce*.

It will take time to prepare this document because each of the attorneys and both of the neutrals will review it and provide input. For example, the financial professional will make sure that your financial goals and interests are reflected in the document and the mental health professional will review your parenting plan and other provisions in the *Agreed Decree of Divorce* to make sure that all of your family goals have been addressed. You and your spouse will also review the draft agreement and your attorneys will make any changes to it that the two of you agree are necessary

Once you have a final *Agreed Decree of Divorce*, you and your spouse will sign it. Then either you and your attorney or your spouse and his attorney will go to court to ask the family law judge to sign it. You and your spouse will both receive a copy of the final signed agreement.

Although your divorce will be official once you have a signed divorce decree, there may still be work left to do in your divorce. For example:

- Legal documents may need to be drafted in order to transfer your interest in certain assets to your former spouse.
- You may have to pay off some of your marital debts and provide your ex and her attorney with proof that you have done so.
- You and your former spouse may have to hire a realtor together to sell your home.
- You may be obligated to purchase medical insurance for your children and your former spouse.
- You may have to buy out your spouse's interest in your joint business.

As appropriate, the members of your team will either help you take care of such tasks or refer to you to someone who can.
Warning! Taking care of the final details in your divorce agreement may take time. So don't become impatient and frustrated. It's essential that you and your spouse do everything that you promised.

Chapter #4, The Role of Your Attorney in Your Collaborative Divorce

During the collaborative divorce process, your attorney will advocate for you and look out for your best interests just as your attorney would do if you were pursuing a litigated divorce. However, the specific roles that your attorney will play in your collaborative divorce will be quite different from the ones that she would play if she were litigating your divorce. For example in a collaborative divorce, your attorney will not negotiate the terms of your divorce for you, battle with your spouse's attorney, try to discredit your spouse, or represent you in court. Instead, working with your spouse's attorney and the mental health and financial professionals on your team, your attorney will help you and your spouse work out the terms of your divorce together by preparing you for your negotiations, facilitating them, and actively participating in them.

This chapter provides an overview of your attorney's role in your divorce. Chapters 2 and 3 provide additional information.

Preparing For Your Collaborative Divorce

Your attorney will spend considerable time before you begin negotiating the terms of your divorce preparing you for the collaborative divorce process. Among other things for example, your attorney will:

- Explain exactly how a collaborative divorce works, including what happens at the team meetings, her role in your divorce, and the roles of the neutral mental health and financial professionals on your team.
- Go over the Participation Agreement with you.

- Make sure that you are clear about your role and responsibilities in your divorce and what it takes to have a successful collaborative divorce. For example, your attorney will explain why it is important that you:

    -- Comply with all of the terms of the Participation Agreement. Your attorney will also tell you what is likely to happen if you don't.
    -- Keep your emotions under control.
    -- Work cooperatively with your spouse.
    -- Focus on your future, not on the failures in your marriage and how your spouse may have contributed to those failures.
    -- Freely share all information related to your divorce with your spouse and with your divorce team.
    -- Complete any homework you may be assigned by a member of your divorce team.
    -- Put the needs of your young children before your own.

- Define and discuss the issues in your divorce.
- Help you identify your divorce interests (and your family's interests) and explain how interest-based negotiating works. For a discussion of interests and interest-based negotiating, turn back to Chapter 2.
- Provide you with a goals worksheet to complete and then talk with you about your answers. If your attorney believes that any of your goals are unrealistic, she will help you rethink them so that you avoid setting yourself up for disappointment and failure when you and your spouse are negotiating the terms of your divorce. Chapter 3 discusses the goals worksheet and you'll find a sample worksheet in the appendix to this book.
- Find out if there are any issues in your divorce that you want settled temporarily while you and your spouse are negotiating permanent solutions to those issues.
- Answer your questions and try to alleviate any concerns you may have regarding the collaborative process, negotiating with your spouse, and so on.

In addition to helping you prepare for your collaborative divorce, your attorney will prepare herself for the process. Prior to the date of your first team meeting for example, your attorney will talk with your spouse's attorney and the neutral professionals to make sure that everyone is on the same page regarding the issues in your divorce, to discuss any problems they think might complicate your negotiations, and if there are any problems to decide how best to handle them. They will also talk about what to put on the agenda for your first team meeting.

After your first team meeting, the two attorneys and the neutral professionals will continue to stay in close contact with one another. They will talk before and after each of your other team meetings, plan what to put on the agenda for each of those meetings, share any information they may have related to your divorce, identify solutions to problems that may develop during your divorce, and actively participate in your negotiations. Although the two attorneys will be looking out for the best interests of their own clients throughout the collaborative process, their relationship will be cooperative, not adversarial.

Working Out the Terms of Your Divorce

During your collaborative divorce, your attorney will do everything possible to help you and your spouse reach a negotiated settlement. Among other things for example, she will:

- Help organize and facilitate your negotiations working with your spouse's attorney and the neutral professionals.
- Provide you with advice and support when you need it.
- Make sure that you have all of the information you need to resolve the issues in your divorce and that you understand that information.
- Help you and your spouse brainstorm solutions to the issues in your divorce together with the rest of your divorce team, including suggesting solutions that may not have occurred to you.
- Help you evaluate each of the solutions that you've identified

in terms of their practical advantages and disadvantages and of how good a job each solution does at satisfying the interests you've identified -- your children's interests, your individual interests and your shared interests -- on both a short-term and a long-term basis. When you are brainstorming and evaluating various solutions to a particular issue, your attorney will draw on her legal background as well as on the knowledge and insights she has gained from working with other couples that ended their marriages through the collaborative process. The mental health and financial professionals will also draw on their own professional backgrounds and previous experiences working with other couples that got collaborative divorces.

- Provide you with legal advice and information when appropriate. However, as you've already learned from reading previous chapters in this book, in a collaborative divorce what the law says about a particular issue you are negotiating serves only as a point of information and reminder of what the final terms of your divorce would probably look like if you and your spouse were not able resolve the issue and had to ask the court to decide it for you. In a collaborative divorce, because it's a non-court process you and your spouse are free to resolve the issue according to what works best for you and your children. However, your attorney will make certain that you don't agree to anything that is illegal.

- Let you know if a provision that you want to include in your divorce agreement will be legally unenforceable, not because you can't include it if you and your spouse both agree to the provision, but because your attorney is obligated to ensure that you have all of the facts that relate to any solution you are considering. It's up to you and your spouse to decide how you want to respond to those facts.

- Help you and your spouse reach an agreement on any issues you can't resolve together. In order to do that your attorney may:

    -- Review your divorce goals and interests with you again as a reminder of what you said was most important to you in your divorce.

-- Help you take another more dispassionate look at the solutions you've already identified.
-- Suggest that you try to identify additional solutions.
-- Suggest new solutions herself.
-- Encourage you to keep negotiating if you're feeling frustrated and want to give up.
-- Explain how a judge (or jury) would probably decide the issue you are stuck on if you decided to take your divorce to court.
-- Suggest that you and your spouse consider hiring a mediator together and inviting the mediator to participate in your next team meeting.

Sharon and Tom Cornwall have three teenagers. In order to ensure that there is consistency in the rules that their children will have to follow after the couple's divorce is final and their children are splitting their time between their parents' homes, the couple has decided to formalize the rules by making them a part of their divorce agreement. After discussing the rules that they want with their individual attorneys as well as with the mental health professional Sharon and Tom agree on rules that address such issues as their children's curfews during the week and on weekends, the amount of TV they can watch on school nights, the amount of time they can be on their phones or texting on school nights, under what conditions they can have parties at their parents' homes, the chores they will be responsible for, and so on.

Both attorneys let the couple know even though they are including the rules in their divorce agreement, the rules won't be legally enforceable. They explain for example, that if Tom changes his mind about their children's curfews, a judge won't force Tom to stick to the curfew time the couple agreed to. Sharon and Tom decide that they want to keep the rules in their agreement anyway because they believe that including them will help underscore their commitment to the rules and make it more likely that they will both stick by them. Knowing that they can include the rules in their agreement underscores Sharon and Tom's satisfaction with the fact that they chose to get a collaborative divorce rather than a litigated divorce.

Before and after each of your team meetings, your attorney will talk with you in-person or by telephone to help prepare you for what's to come. For example, she will discuss what happened at your last team meeting to make sure that you are happy with any decisions you may have made at the meeting and to find out about any concerns that you may have; she will explain what is going to happen at the next team meeting and help you prepare for it; she will discuss anything she feels you may need to do in order to be a more effective participant in your divorce negotiations; and she will try to get a sense of how you are doing emotionally.

If your attorney learns during your collaborative divorce that you've violated one of the terms of your Participation Agreement, she will talk with you about what you've done, explain why it's wrong and how your violation could harm the process. If the violation was unintentional and relatively minor -- most violations are -- your attorney will explain what you should have done differently. However, if your violation appears to be intentional and is more serious -- you deliberately did something to give yourself an advantage in your divorce -- your attorney will give you an opportunity to correct what you did. If you refuse to do so, she will explain again why it's important that you comply with each and every provision of the Participation Agreement and remind you of the fact that when you signed the agreement you acknowledged that if you were unable or unwilling to abide by it, your attorney would be obligated to end your collaborative divorce and withdraw from your case. If you are like most spouses in your same situation, you'll correct your error because you are committed to the collaborative divorce process and want it to succeed.

After you and your spouse have reached an agreement on all of the issues in your divorce, your attorney, working with your spouse's attorney, will prepare a draft of your divorce agreement or draft decree, based on the solutions you and your spouse agreed to during your negotiations and then they will share the draft with the two neutrals on your team. As necessary, the attorneys will revise the draft based on the neutrals' feedback. Then the attorney will share the draft with you and your spouse so that you have an opportunity to review and comment on it. Once everyone is happy with the way the agreement is worded, the attorneys will finalize the document and one of them will submit it to the court for its approval.

Given that the two attorneys will have shared the agreement with you and your spouse only after everyone on your team agrees that it accurately reflects everything that you and your spouse agreed to, it's unlikely that the two of you will have any significant problems with the draft and that there will be any delays in completing your divorce. Figure 4.1 illustrates how this approach to drafting your final decree contrasts with the way it's done in a litigated divorce.

Once the court has signed the decree and made your divorce official, your attorney will review with you any actions you must take in order to comply with the final terms of your divorce. If your attorney or another member of your divorce team cannot help you handle these final details, they will refer you to someone who can. Chapter 3 reviews some of the actions former spouses must often take once their divorce is final.

Figure 4.1, Comparing the Final Divorce Decree Drafting Process in a Collaborative and a Litigated Divorce

John and Sue Swartz are getting divorced. Preparing their divorce decree -- the written document that spells out all of the final terms of their divorce and that is submitted to the court for its approval -- will be a lot easier, less contentious and a lot less time consuming depending on whether they decide to use the collaborative process to end their marriage or they pursue a litigated divorce. The following two anecdotes help illustrate why.

If John and Sue get a collaborative divorce:

Once John and Sue have reached an agreement on all of the issues in their divorce, John's lawyer prepares a first draft of the couple's *decree of divorce* and sends the draft to Sue's attorney and to the mental health and financial professionals on the couple's divorce team, all of whom review the draft decree. The two neutrals send their proposed changes to John's attorney and then the lawyers meet to review the document together and to redraft portions of it as necessary. Once everyone on the couple's divorce team is happy with the draft decree, John and Sue review it and suggest their own changes. They want to make have minimal changes to the document and neither of them have any problem with the changes that they each ask for.

If John and Sue get a litigated divorce:

Once John and Sue are okay with the agreement that their attorneys have worked out for them, John's lawyer sends the decree he has drafted to John for his review. After making the changes that John asks for, his lawyer sends the decree to Sue's lawyer, who reviews it and asks for some changes in the document. When John's lawyer reviews those changes with his client, John is immediately suspicious of them because he assumes that the changes will benefit Sue at his expense. Therefore, even though his attorney has no problem with the changes because they simply tighten up the language in the couple's draft decree to make sure that the terms of their divorce are absolutely clear, John refuses to go along with them. Therefore, his lawyer tells Sue's lawyer that he can't agree to the changes. In response, Sue's lawyer files a motion with the court to accept the decree with the changes and John's lawyer responds by filing a motion asking the court to accept the decree without the changes. A court hearing on the motions is held and at the end of the hearing the judge decides what to do.

Chapter #5, The Role of the Mental Health Professional in Your Collaborative Divorce

The mental health professional will play multiple key roles in your collaborative divorce. First, she'll act as a neutral advocate for you and your spouse by staying attuned to the kinds of support and assistance you may need individually and as a couple during the collaborative process so that each of you can be at your best during your divorce. Second, she will serve as a neutral advocate for your children to ensure that you and your spouse keep their needs front and center during your negotiations. Among other things for example, she will help you develop a parenting plan that reflects their interests, supports family interaction, and includes a parenting schedule that makes sense for your entire family. Although your kids won't have seats at your divorce negotiating table, the mental health professional will act as their proxy. Third, the mental health professional will be your teacher, teaching you and your spouse communication and negotiation skills and helping the two of you deal with any emotions that may be making it more difficult for you to focus on the business of settling the issues in your divorce. Finally, the mental health professional will be a neutral advocate for the collaborative process itself, constantly assessing how well it's working and intervening if the process begins to go off course.

The rest of this chapter provides more specific information about the mental health professional's involvement in your divorce. It also includes a detailed discussion of parenting plans.

Assessing Your Needs

Early in your divorce the mental health professional will meet with you and your spouse individually and maybe as a couple. She'll want to get to know each of you -- your personal histories, how your emotions may be getting in the way of your good judgment, your communication skills, the issues that worry you the most about getting divorced, what you want from your divorce, your divorce hot buttons, the dynamics of your relationship with your spouse, including how the two of you have communicated with one another in the past, and the future you each envision for yourselves after your divorce.

The mental health professional will use what she learns from talking to you and your spouse as well as whatever she learns from the two attorneys and the financial professional to figure out the kinds of help you may need from her individually and/or as a couple in order for you to be able to participate successfully in the collaborative divorce process. Also, throughout your divorce, she will stay attuned to how well you are doing emotionally and how well you and your spouse are communicating with one another, and she'll provide you with the advice and support you may need to move the process forward.

Tip. When you talk with the mental health professional don't withhold or mischaracterize information about yourself or your marriage because you're embarrassed or ashamed about it -- your spouse is abusive, you have a drinking problem, and so on. The mental health professional needs the straight scoop. Furthermore, you can be assured that you won't be the first spouse the mental health professional has worked with who has problems like yours.

Helping You Handle Your Emotions

Getting divorced is one of life's most emotionally difficult experiences, so it's no surprise that sometimes your emotions may get the best of you during your collaborative divorce. When that happens, the mental health professional will try to help you get a handle on your emotions so that they will have less control over you. It's important not to let them get out of hand because if they do, you may be at risk for saying and doing things that could upset your spouse, jeopardize the collaborative process, and worse case scenario, even cause it to end. By not allowing your emotions to get the best of you, you'll be better able to get your points across to your spouse, to focus on your future, to think clearly and to make good decisions about the terms of your divorce.

Warning! In her neutral role, the mental health professional will not act as your therapist. Therefore, if you need more help than she can provide, she'll give you the names of some therapists you may want to work with. If you are already working with a therapist, the mental health professional may ask you for permission to discuss your divorce with him.

Warning! Many divorcing spouses feel entitled to be angry with their husband or wife, maybe because they are in shock over the fact that their marriage is ending and why it's ending or because they feel victimized. The *righteous anger* makes it impossible for them to see both sides of the issues in their divorce and as a result, negotiating a mutually acceptable settlement agreement is much more difficult.

Tip: You have the right to be angry and upset about your divorce. However, if you have intense anger problems, you may need one-on-one therapy before you can use the collaborative divorce process successfully.

If the mental health professional learns that you have something going on in your life that is likely to impair your judgment and interfere with your ability to make good decisions during your divorce, like an untreated alcohol or drug problem for example, she will urge you to get help with your problem/s and she'll talk with you about your options for receiving the help you need. It's important that you and your spouse be at your best during your collaborative divorce because it takes a lot of mental and emotional energy to get through the process and you won't have the energy you need if you are struggling with emotional problems, addictions, and so on.

The mental health professional may also suggest that you and your spouse agree to put your divorce on hold for a while so that you get the help that you need without having to worry about working out the terms of your divorce. If either of you baulks at the suggestion, the mental health professional will explain why it's in your best interest to take a break for a while. In the end however, whether or not you do will be up to you and your spouse and sometimes when spouses choose not to, they are still able to have a successful collaborative divorce.

Joan and Will Lewis are getting a collaborative divorce, but Joan is so angry about Will's affair (She discovered the affair after finding another woman's underwear in her laundry.), that she can't see anything from her husband's perspective. As a result, the couple's negotiations are going nowhere. However, Joan's attorney and the mental health professional convince Joan that she needs to go to therapy and the couple agrees to halt their divorce for one month. Once they resume their divorce negotiations, it's obvious that the therapy has helped Joan with her anger. As a result, the couple is able to complete their collaborative divorce.

Early in the divorce of Libby and Randall Kilpatrick, the couple learns that Abby, one of their daughters, has cancer and must receive many rounds of chemotherapy. Abby's chemo does not go well however and so she keeps ending up in the hospital, which causes some delays in the couple's divorce. Even so the couple is able to make progress on working out the terms of their divorce. Late in their divorce however, when Libby and Randall have just one more team meeting left, Abby is hospitalized for ten days. The professionals on Libby and Randall's divorce team become very concerned that the couple will be so exhausted from having to be at the hospital all of the time and from the stress of worrying about Abby that they won't be able to make the remaining decisions about their divorce at their final team meeting. Therefore, they urge the couple to reschedule that meeting so that they will have some time to rest first. Libby and Randall refuse however and explain that the stress of not completing their divorce would be worse than pushing forward despite their fatigue. So the final team meeting is held as scheduled and happily, Libby and Randall are able to resolve all of the remaining issues in their divorce.

Helping You Become A Better Communicator

Good communication is essential to the success of the collaborative process. You must be able to clearly explain your goals and interests to your spouse and the team, participate in the give and take of the negotiation process, and be a good listener. Therefore, if you're having problems getting your points across or if you are tuning out your spouse or misinterpreting his comments, the mental health professional will work with you to improve your communication skills. Among other things she may:

- Make you aware of any words and phrases you may be using that are pushing your spouse's emotional hot buttons and help you choose more effective ways to get your points across. Your choice of words can make it easier for your spouse to accept what you are saying.
- Help you convey your thoughts more effectively and clarify your comments. For example, the mental health professional may ask you, "Are you saying XYZ? " or "Help us understand your concern. It sounds like what you're actually worried about is ABC. Am I right?"
- Teach you how to be an active listener. Active listening involves hearing what your spouse is really saying -- the true meaning behind your spouse's words. It requires that you pay close attention to your spouse's words and body language without interrupting him or judging his comments. Active listening also requires that you respect your spouse's opinions and needs although it doesn't require that you agree with your spouse's point of view.
- Make you aware of the negative message your tone of voice may be sending to your spouse and help you speak in a more neutral tone so that your spouse will be more receptive to hearing and acting on what you are saying. You may be sending a negative message because your tone of voice is sarcastic, irritated, belittling, or angry, for example.

When necessary, the mental health professional will also sensitize you to the negative messages your body language may be conveying to your spouse. For example, whenever your spouse speaks you may sigh visibly, look away, tap your fingers on the table, or watch the clock as though you can't wait for him to be quiet.

Tip. During your team meetings, take note of how the two attorneys and the two neutrals relate to one another and to you and your spouse. They will be modeling the kinds of behaviors that you may need to adopt in order for your collaborative divorce to be a success -- clear, respectful communication, active listening, and joint problem solving, for example.

Shannon and Ed Riley are a young couple who are getting a collaborative divorce. They are having a very difficult time communicating with one another about their children outside of their divorce negotiations and their conversations typically end in arguments and bad feelings. Their communication problems are complicating their divorce because they arrive at each of their team meetings feeling very stressed out, frustrated with one another, and angry. As a result, their team members are having to spend a lot of time trying to help them resolve the emotional fall out from their communications problems and so Shannon and Ed's divorce is not moving forward as quickly the couple hoped it would. They want to communicate with one another more productively, but they have no idea how to do that. Therefore, their attorneys ask the mental health professional if she would create a "playbook" for their clients -- a simple written communication guide that each spouse could keep in front of him or herself when the couple is trying to have a conversation outside of their team meetings.

The mental health professional agrees to create the playbook for the couple and then teaches Shannon and Ed how to use it. The playbook does the job. It helps the couple improve their ability to communicate with one another and eventually Shannon and Ed are able to talk with one another about difficult topics like their children and issues in their divorce without having to use the playbook. You can download a sample playbook similar to the one that the mental health professional created for Shannon and Ed at www.vmjames.com.

Helping You Help Your Kids

As this book has already made clear, there are many reasons why divorce can be emotionally devastating for young children. For example:

- Their family structure may collapse as a result of their parents' divorce.
- Their parents' parenting abilities may become diminished and so their parents may no longer be able to meet their needs.
- Their parents may use them as pawns in their divorce.
- Their parents may turn them into their confidants.

If you and your spouse have young children, one of the mental health professional's primary goals will be to help you help them get through your divorce emotionally unscathed. Among other things therefore, she will make sure that you are clear about what you should never do around your children -- make disparaging comments about your spouse, share your worries about your divorce with them, interfere in their ability to spend quality time with your spouse, undermine or denigrate your spouse's parenting decisions, for example -- and she'll explain the importance of demonstrating through your words and deeds that you are still a family and that you and your spouse will always be there for them.

If you and your spouse have a disagreement about your children during your divorce and you can't resolve it on your own, the mental health professional will try to help you work it out together or may suggest that you discuss the problem with your entire team in order to benefit from everyone's feedback. She may also recommend that the two of you work with a family therapist.

The mental health professional may also meet with your children one-on-one or all together so she can hear directly from them how they feel about your divorce, what they are afraid of and what they need from you that they may not be getting. In addition, she may meet with you and your spouse and your children so your children can share their thoughts with you and so that you and your spouse can tell them about how you'll work together as parents during and after your divorce and what you'll do to help them.

One of the most important ways that the mental health professional will help you help your kids is by working with you and your spouse on the preparation of your parenting plan, which will be part of your final divorce decree. A parenting plan is a detailed written blueprint that lays out exactly how the two of you will raise your children together after your divorce and that spells out your individual and joint responsibilities and decision-making rights. Working out all of these issues together with the help of the mental health professional and putting all of your decisions down on paper will help minimize the likelihood that any kid-related problems will develop between you and your spouse after you are divorced and will make it easier for the two of you to maintain the integrity of your family. Furthermore, if problems do develop, the details of your parenting plan will make it easier for the two of you to resolve them. The next section of this chapter discusses parenting plans in detail.

The mental health professional may ask that a child specialist be added to your divorce team. A child specialist is a mental health professional who specializes in working with children and counsels them and their parents. The child specialist may have suggestions for things to include in your parenting plan that will make it easier for your children to adjust to the changes that your divorce will bring to their lives.

Donna and Nash Harvey are working on their parenting plan. Thirteen-year old Josh is their only child. They told Josh about their divorce two months ago, shortly after they decided to end their marriage. During a meeting with the mental health professional on their collaborative divorce team, Donna and Nash mention how worried they are about their son because his behavior had changed recently. They explain that he has begun spending an unusual amount of time alone in his room and although he has always been a talkative child, he's not talking to them very much anymore. The couple doesn't understand why Josh is acting as he is and they are not sure how to respond. The mental health professional suggests that they bring Josh to their next meeting with her. Donna and Nash agree.

A few days before the date of that meeting, Donna calls the mental health professional to find out if there is any point in having Josh attend it because Josh had told her that he didn't want to talk at the meeting. The mental health professional says that she would like Josh to come to the meeting anyway.

When the day of the meeting arrives and the four of them get together, everyone chats casually for a little while to give Josh an opportunity to relax a bit. The mental health professional also explains to Josh why she wanted him to be at the meeting and asks if he would be willing to talk with her one-on-one. Josh says that he would.

The mental health professional and Josh spend some time talking by themselves about his parents' divorce. Eventually, Josh becomes comfortable enough to tell her that he is mad at his parents because their divorce is disrupting his life and because he feels like they are so caught up in their divorce that they are not considering its affect on him. He says that he doesn't feel like his parents are there for him right now and is afraid that they won't be there for him after their divorce either. Josh says that he wants his relationship with his parents to be like it was before they began their divorce. The mental health professional and Josh talk more about his fears and about what he needs from his parents. Before they finish their conversation, she asks Josh if he is willing to share with his parents what he has just shared with her when they all get together again. Josh says he will try.

Once everyone is back in the same room, the mental health professional lets Donna and Nash know that Josh wants to talk to them about how their divorce is affecting him and what they can do to make him feel safer and happier. The couple listens intently while Josh speaks to them and it's obvious from the looks on their faces that they feel terrible that they have made him so sad. After Josh stops talking, Donna and Nash tell him how much they love him and how sorry they are that their divorce has been so difficult for him. They also apologize for letting him down. Then, the mental health professional asks Josh to tell his parents what they can do to make him feel better.

By the end of the meeting Donna and Nash have committed to giving Josh what he needs from them and Josh understands that going forward the three of them will work together as a family just like they used to. He feels better now that his parents have listened to him and are committed to making him feel safer and happier.

Helping With Your Parenting Plan

You, your spouse and the mental health professional will begin working on your parenting plan early in your divorce. Most of the work will be done outside your team meetings.

The plan will spell out exactly how the two of you will raise your children together after your marriage is officially over and will detail your individual and joint parental rights and responsibilities. Once you have a draft plan, you will bring it to a team meeting so that you can discuss it with everyone on your team and so that they can help you finalize it. You can download a sample-parenting plan at www.vmjames.com. However, your plan may be a lot different than the sample.

Before you begin writing your plan, the mental health professional will talk with you and your spouse about the importance of thinking of yourselves as co-parents, not as a divorced husband and wife. Although the distinction may seem minor, there is actually a powerful difference between the two terms. The term "divorced husband and wife" conjures up an image of parents who don't communicate with one another very much about their kids and who may be in constant conflict over them; the term "co-parents" on the other hand implies that both parents are working together to raise their kids. In other words, thinking of yourselves as co-parents will help you and your spouse avoid remaining caught up in the emotions and problems that led you to a divorce and will make it easier for the two of you to maintain the right mindset for raising happy, emotionally secure children, will make it easier for you to respect and honor one another as parents, and will minimize the potential for conflict over your kids.

At the start of the plan development process, the mental health professional will ask you to complete some exercises intended to help you begin thinking about what you want to include in your plan. For example, she may ask you to:

- Talk with one another about your post-divorce parenting goals and interests.
- Discuss the rights of children.
- Write a co-parenting mission statement.
- List any holidays or annual family events that are particularly important to you -- the family reunion you attend every

summer, your children's birthday, or your own birthday, for example.

• Identify any special family traditions you both want to continue after your marriage ends.

At a minimum your parenting plan will address:

• How you'll share custody of your minor children and parenting time, including when your children will be with each of you during the week and on weekends.

• How you'll handle custody and parenting time if one of you moves out of the area.

• How (or whether) your parenting schedule will change when your children are on summer break or when they have other vacations from school.

• Your individual and shared parental rights and duties, including how you will make decisions about your children, like the after-school activities they'll participate in, the religion they'll be raised in, the Summer camp they'll attend, whether they will go to public or private schools, and so on. You and your spouse may decide to share some kinds of decision-making and you may agree that each of you will have the right to make certain types of decisions by yourselves when the children are with you.

• How you'll handle childcare issues. For example, will they attend daycare, will they have a nanny, or will one of your parents take care of them? Also, if they go to daycare, how will the facility be chosen and if they have a nanny, how will you select that person?

• How you will share such costs as the cost of your children's health insurance and out-of-pocket medical expenses, their private school and college tuitions, the expenses related to your children's after-school activities, Summer camp, lessons, and so on.

• The role of your significant others in your children's lives. For example, when if ever will it be appropriate for one of your girlfriends or boyfriends to sleep over at your home when your children are there, to go on a vacation with your kids, to take care of them, and so on.

- How you'll accommodate your children's changing needs as they grow up.
- How you will take care of any special needs your kids may have.
- The measures you and your spouse will take to minimize your children's exposure to any conflict between the two of you.
- How the two of you will resolve any parenting-related disputes outside of court. Your plan will probably state that you will try to work out your differences on your own and if that doesn't work, that you'll meet with a marital therapist, your religious advisor or with a parenting coordinator. (A parenting coordinator is a mental health professional who has received special training to help divorced parents communicate when they are having problems resolving issues related to their children or when they have to make difficult decisions about them. Working with a parenting coordinator makes it less likely that parents will have to get a full modification of their parenting plan because they can't reach an agreement on the issue/s they disagree about.) Your parenting plan may also state that if your meeting with a marital therapist, your religious advisor or with a parenting coordinator fails to resolve your differences, you'll return to the collaborative process or try mediation.

Tip. If you and your spouse are separated, you may have a temporary custody and parenting plan in place when you begin working on your permanent plan. You and your spouse can agree to make the terms of the temporary plan permanent, change certain aspects of the plan, or add new provisions to it.

Chapter #6, The Role of the Financial Professional in Your Collaborative Divorce

It doesn't matter whether you and your spouse are worth $50,000 or $50 million, deciding what to do about the assets and debts from your marriage and resolving other money-related matters is a very important part of your divorce. The advice and assistance of the financial professional on your team will be invaluable when you are making such decisions.

After reading previous chapters in this book, you should already have a good understanding of the financial professional's role in your divorce. This chapter summarizes much of that information and offers additional details to give you a more complete look at how the financial professional will help you. It begins by reviewing the basic financial issues that are a part of most divorces. Then it details how the financial professional will prepare you to address those issues and explains some of the ways that he may help you wrap up any final financial details you may need to tend to once your divorce is official.

The Financial Issues in Your Divorce

The financial professional on your team will help you and your spouse define and understand the financial issues you must resolve before your divorce can be final. Although no divorce is exactly alike, those issues will probably include:

- How you'll divvy up the assets and debts from your marriage. The more assets you own and/or the more debts you owe, the more difficult it will probably be to make these decisions. However, couples who don't have many assets can also have difficulty deciding how to divide up their assets because both spouses may believe that they each need the few assets that they own.

At some point in the process, the attorneys will explain that Texas is a community property state, which means that you and your spouse each have an undivided interest in the value of your marital assets (These are the assets that either of you acquired during your marriage, but not any assets that either of you may have inherited or received as gifts during that time.) as well as an undivided obligation to pay your marital debts with some specific exceptions. In other words, in Texas both of you own all of your assets and owe all of your debts regardless of who purchased the assets during your marriage and who incurred the debts, with some specific exceptions. The financial professional will help you develop options for sharing your marital assets and debts given your interests and economic realities.

- Whether one of you will pay child support to the other and if so, the amount of the support. Although Texas has a formula for establishing the monthly amount of support to be paid, you and your spouse can agree on a different amount as well as a process for paying the support.
- The extras you want your children to have after your divorce and how you'll pay for them. Those extras might include private school, dance lessons, private tutoring, Summer camp, college, and so on. You'll be asked to consider not only your children's current expenses, but also to anticipate their future expenses given that as your children grow older their expenses will change, and to decide as best you can, how you will handle them.

Tip. Some parents fund their children's extras by setting up a joint bank account and making regular contributions to the account according to an agreed-upon funding method.

- How you'll ensure that your minor children will have health coverage after your marriage ends. Although you'll probably agree to maintain their current coverage, you may decide to change their coverage if you and your spouse both agree that the change would be in your children's best interest.

- What you will do about your own health insurance, if you are currently on your spouse's policy. Your options include:

    -- Purchasing an individual policy and paying for it yourself.
    -- Purchasing an individual policy that your spouse pays for.
    -- Remaining on your spouse's policy temporarily. Under COBRA, a federal law, you may be entitled to stay on the policy for a certain number of months after your divorce is final. However, you'll have to pay the full cost of the coverage because your spouse's employer will no longer subsidize the cost of insuring you, and so your COBRA coverage won't be cheap.
    -- Enrolling in your employer's health insurance plan, if it has one.

- Whether one of you will pay support to the other and if so, the amount of the support and its duration. If you have been a stay-at-home Mom or Dad during your marriage for example, you may want to receive some support so that you can afford to upgrade your job skills and qualify for a good job, or you and your spouse may agree that while your children are young, you should receive enough spousal support that you can afford to stay at home with them.

Skip and Jana Pauley are struggling with how to ensure that Jana has health insurance after her divorce. Skip is a software developer and Jana is a self-employed graphic designer. Right now, she is insured through Skip's job. Today they are meeting with the financial professional on their team to evaluate each of the options they identified at a previous meeting. Those options are:

#1.   Through COBRA, Jana will remain on Skip's policy for as long as she can.

> *#2.   Jana will purchase an individual health policy.*
> *# 3.   Skip will pay the cost of Jana's individual insurance policy*
> *#4.   Jana will find a job that provides her with health insurance.*

They begin to discuss each option one by one. Jana says that she doesn't like the first option because it's only a temporary solution to her problem and because the cost of the coverage will be high so she will have to cut back substantially in other areas of her budget to afford it. However, she doesn't eliminate Option #1.

Jana mentions that she looked into the cost of getting her own individual policy; but it's going to be expensive and she has not found an insurance company that will cover her asthma. However she has just learned about an organization called the Freelancers Union, which offers their members group insurance. So she is going to look into becoming a union member and getting coverage through it. Jana goes on to say that if the union coverage turns out not to be a viable option, she'll look for a job that provides health coverage. However, if she gets a job, she wants to try to keep her freelance business going on the side.

Skip mentions that he has reviewed his post-divorce budget and is willing to pay the cost of Jana's COBRA coverage for up to six months in order to give her time to figure out what she is going to do about insurance coverage. Jana says that if she has not gotten her own health insurance by the time the six months are up, she will either pick up the cost of the remaining months of COBRA coverage so she can stay on Skip's policy a little longer, or she will purchase her own insurance, even if it won't cover her asthma. Jana and Skip are both happy with this arrangement.

Getting the Preliminaries Out of the Way

Before the financial professional can help you resolve the financial issues in your divorce, he'll meet with you and your spouse individually and maybe together too. During the meetings he will gather initial information about your finances, assess how much you know about your family's finances and try to understand the dynamics of your relationship with one another, especially your money relationship. For example, do you make most of the financial decisions in your marriage, have the two of you always made every decision related to your finances together, or do you make some decisions and your spouse makes the others? The financial professional will also gauge how well the two of you are getting along, whether you appear to trust one another, and whether there are any financial hot buttons in your divorce. The financial professional will use this information to help him define the financial issues in your divorce and to determine the kinds of help you are likely to need from him before and during your divorce negotiations so that you can resolve those issues.

The financial professional will learn more about your finances by asking you and your spouse to provide him with various financial documents and other information. Figure 3.2 in Chapter 3 summarizes the kinds of information he'll want.

He will also help you and your spouse prepare budgets for your lives after divorce so that you both have a clear idea going into your negotiations of how much it's probably going to cost you to live once your marriage ends. If you have children, he'll also help you develop a budget for them too. The budget will be very helpful when you are discussing child support and writing your parenting plan because it will provide you with a realistic understanding of what it will cost to raise your kids and will make it easier for you to figure out which extras you can afford to give them, if any.

Juanita and Dan Fernandez have three children. They are ending their 20-year marriage and are grappling with the issue of what to do about their children's expenses. Their children are involved in a lot of extracurricular activities and the couple wants them to be able to continue doing those things after their divorce. However, they are not sure about the best way to share the cost of those activities and how to actually pay for each one.

To help them decide, the financial professional asks Juanita and Dan to create an itemized list of all of their children's current expenses. They complete that exercise with no problem, but they begin struggling when the financial professional asks them to brainstorm options for how to pay for each expense. Every time one of them suggests something the other spouse rejects it. Juanita and Dan begin feeling very frustrated and Dan even wonders aloud whether they should turn to the court for help. At that point, the financial professional suggests that they end the meeting and get together again the following week with him and their attorneys. He wants the attorneys to talk with the couple about how the court would decide the issue of their children's expenses. At that next meeting the attorneys remind the couple that if they can't work out the issue of their children's expenses through the collaborative process, the process will end and Juanita and Dan will have to hire new attorneys. They also explain that the court will use a standardized table that takes into account the number of children in their family to determine the basic amount of money one of them must pay the other in child support and that the table will not reflect the individual needs of their children. If Juanita and Dan want their children to have more than the table provides for, their new attorneys will have to try to negotiate something for them or they'll have to ask the court to decide the issue. The attorneys also warn that it's not uncommon in such a situation for couples to end up back in court after their divorce is over asking for modifications to their support agreements.

After hearing from their attorneys, Juanita and Dan decide that they really need to work out their own agreement, so they schedule another meeting with the financial professional. This time they identify three options:

#1. *Juanita will pay certain expenses and Dan will pay others.*
#2. *They will add up all of the expenses and Juanita and Dan will each pay half.*
#3. *They will each pay a pro rata share of the total cost of their children's expenses based on their individual annual incomes.*

After a lot of discussion, the couple decides that option #3 is fairest given that Juanita makes considerably more than Dan does. Next, they discuss how they will actually pay for each expense. One option is for Juanita and Dan to write separate checks for their share of an expense and to be responsible for ensuring that their payments are made by the applicable due dates. However, Dan doesn't like this option because Juanita is not a good money manager and she travels a lot for her job, so he is concerned that sometimes she may forget to pay her share of some of the expenses. After some discussion, they decide that a better option would be for the couple to open a joint checking account for their children's expenses and at the start of every quarter for each of them to deposit their share of the expenses that will have to be paid during that quarter. Then, Dan will write checks for each expense as they come due and will provide Juanita with an accounting at the end of each quarter together with a list of the amounts due for the next quarter. The couple likes this arrangement because it will ensure the timely payment of their children's expenses and because it reflects their individual money management abilities.

Once the financial professional has reviewed all of your financial information, he will talk with each of you together or separately about the state of your finances and their implications for your divorce agreement so that he can help each of you have a realistic view of what is and isn't possible in your divorce. This is an especially important conversation if the financial professional believes that one or both of you is in denial about the state of your family's finances -- you think that your spouse can afford to pay you more in spousal support than he can or that you are going to exit your marriage with more assets than you probably will, for example. Although your spouse may have already tried to give you a financial reality check, you may have dismissed his comments because you didn't want to hear the truth or because you don't take seriously anything he says to you anymore. However, you may be more receptive to hearing and accepting the truth if it comes from the financial professional, who has no financial stake in your divorce, no emotional ties to you, who is an unbiased participant in your divorce, and who can clearly convey the facts to you.

Resolving the Financial Issues in Your Divorce

When you and your spouse begin negotiating the financial terms of your divorce, the financial professional will:

- Make sure that you are clear about the financial issues in your divorce.

- Help you identify as many solutions as possible for resolving those issues.
- Ensure that you and your spouse understand the pros and cons of each solution and how each solution would work. For example, the financial professional may explain the tax consequences of certain solutions, prepare financial projections to help you appreciate how different solutions will affect you and/or your children in the years to come, and help you evaluate the solutions in light of the budgets you've prepared.
- Suggest that you consult with other financial professionals, like a CPA, realtor, insurance broker, and so on.
- Help you and your spouse together with your attorneys negotiate a final resolution to each of the financial issues in your divorce.

Throughout the negotiating process, the financial professional will try to help you avoid making decisions that might work for you in the short term, but are not in your best interest long term. For example, if you are determined to keep your home, you may decide that you'll come up with the money you need to pay your spouse her share of the equity in your home by borrowing against the money in your 401(k) plan. However, assuming that you are younger than 59 1/2, the financial professional will explain that if you take money out of that plan and you don't repay all of it within five years, you'll have to pay a 10% penalty on the unpaid balance. In addition, because the IRS will treat as income the money that you withdraw, you'll be taxed on whatever you don't repay, which will increase your federal income tax liability. Furthermore, if you can't afford to pay the IRS what you owe in taxes, you'll end up in hot water with Uncle Sam, which could be very costly. In addition, the financial professional will warn you that if you don't repay the money, you'll have less to live on once you retire. Although that may not be of concern to you if you are young and have plenty of years to rebuild the balance in your 401(k), if you're just years away from retirement, tapping the money in the account could be disastrous for your long-term financial security and might even force you to have to change your retirement plans.

After You've Worked Everything Out

After you and your spouse have settled all of the financial issues in your divorce and a judge has signed your divorce decree, the financial professional will help you tie up the loose ends in your divorce. For example, he may refer you to:

- An estate planning attorney. If you have an estate plan, the attorney will help you revise the provisions of the plan that need to be changed now that your marriage has ended. You'll need to legally designate who you want to inherit the assets that you had earmarked in your will for your former spouse, for example. To do that you'll either need to write a new will or amend your existing will by preparing a document called a *codicil*. And, if your spouse was the beneficiary of your living trust, you'll need to revise the trust agreement as well. In addition, if your former spouse had power of attorney for your finances and/or your health care during your marriage, you'll probably want to give those important responsibilities to someone else. Finally, if you don't have an estate plan, the estate-planning attorney can help you prepare one.
- A financial planner. The planner can help you manage your finances, put a savings plan in place, make sound investments, plan for your retirement, and so on. In addition, this person can help with all of the paperwork that will have to be completed to transfer any assets as part of your divorce agreement.
- An insurance broker. The broker can evaluate your current insurance coverage and advise you about any changes he recommends. For example, the broker may suggest that you purchase additional life insurance, renter's insurance if you are renting a place to live, disability insurance if you work for yourself, and long-term care insurance if you are in your mid to late fifties and don't have another way to finance a possible stay in a nursing home.

Appendix

COLLABORATIVE LAW
PARTICIPATION AGREEMENT

PURPOSE

[FULLNAME1] and [FULLNAME2] ("the Clients") have chosen to use the collaborative law process to resolve their family differences. [FIRSTNAME1] is represented by [LAWYER1]. [FIRSTNAME2] is represented by [LAWYER2]. The "Collaborative Team" consists of the collaborative lawyers together with any additional collaborative professionals who sign participation agreements. We adopt this conflict resolution process, which relies on honesty, cooperation, and professionalism geared toward the future well-being of the restructured family. Our goal is to eliminate the negative economic, social and emotional consequences of litigation. We commit to the collaborative law process to resolve differences with the goal of achieving a resolution that is acceptable to the clients under the circumstances.

COMMITMENTS

We commit to a collaborative problem-solving process which is based on:

1. Identification of the goals and interests of each client;
2. The Clients' empowerment to make decisions;
3. Full disclosure of relevant information;
4. The collaborative lawyers' assistance to their respective clients in identifying issues, analyzing relevant information, developing options, and understanding consequences; and
5. The lawyers' commitment to the Protocols of Practice for Collaborative Family Lawyers promulgated by the Collaborative Law Institute of Texas, Inc.

OTHER COLLABORATIVE PROFESSIONALS, EXPERTS AND ADVISORS

Unless otherwise agreed in writing, if other collaborative professionals, experts or advisors (hereinafter sometimes referred to as "consultants") are needed, they will be engaged jointly as neutrals. The Clients may engage consultants for purposes of communication facilitation, financial and tax advice, valuation, cash flow analysis, [resolution of parenting issues,] and assistance with any other issue that requires specialized or expert advice and/or recommendations. The Clients will agree in advance how consultants will be paid. Unless the Clients, collaborative lawyers, and consultants agree otherwise in writing, the consultants engaged are disqualified from testifying as fact or expert witnesses, and their writings are inadmissible in a judicial proceeding between the Clients. This disqualification does not apply to individuals engaged by the Clients to assist them in other matters independent of the collaborative law process, such as preparation of tax returns and estate planning. Nothing contained herein precludes a collaborative lawyer from consulting with other professionals as necessary to better understand the factual and legal issues presented in the case.

Consultants may communicate with Clients, the lawyers, other consultants engaged in the collaborative law process, and any lawyer consulted for a second opinion during the collaborative law process.

Once a neutral consultant has been engaged to serve as a member of the Collaborative Team and has signed a Participation Agreement, neither client may unilaterally terminate his or her services. A request to remove or replace such a consultant will be an agenda item for discussion by the entire Collaborative Team. Insistence upon terminating such services may be grounds for the termination of the collaborative law process. The Clients may agree to the termination of the services of such a consultant and the replacement with another consultant to serve on the Collaborative Team. This provision does not prohibit either client from unilaterally substituting a new collaborative lawyer as his or her lawyer.

COMMUNICATION

Constructive and Respectful Communication. We agree to effectively and honestly communicate with each other. All written and verbal communications will be respectful and constructive. Joint meetings will focus on those issues necessary to the constructive resolution of the matter. We agree not to engage in unnecessary discussions of past events.

Settlement Discussions. The Clients agree to discuss settlement with each other only in the joint meetings, unless they agree otherwise. A request to discontinue any such discussion outside of a joint meeting will be immediately honored. Settlement issues will not be discussed at unannounced times in any manner. The lawyers plan agendas for settlement meetings and draft or review documents, but no agreements will be made by the lawyers on behalf of the Clients.

Electronic and Written Communication. The Clients authorize the use of unencrypted email, facsimile, or any other electronic communications to relay information and deliver documents in the collaborative law process. Joint communications of agendas, minutes, drafts of documents and agreements may be sent simultaneously to the Clients and the Collaborative Team.

Transparent Communication. If a client sends any written communication to the other client's collaborative lawyer, the client will copy his or her own lawyer with the communication. A written communication sent by a collaborative lawyer to the other client will be copied to the client's collaborative lawyer. A collaborative lawyer shall forward promptly to the other lawyer all client-to-client communications received.

Written Team Communication. In order to facilitate the process, there are times that the Collaborative Team may engage in written internal communications intended only for the Collaborative Team. A written communication designated as a "team communication" will not be communicated to the Clients.

Collaborative Law Process Participation Agreement (Rev. 3/07)
© Collaborative Law Institute of Texas, Inc. 2004

Include the next two paragraphs if a minor child is involved:
Communications Regarding Children. The Clients acknowledge that inappropriate communications can be harmful to their child[ren]. Communication with the minor child[ren] regarding the case will occur only as agreed by the Clients.

Our goal is to reach an agreement that promotes the best interests of the child[ren]. No client will unilaterally seek a custody evaluation while the matter is in the collaborative law process. No member of the Collaborative Team will interview the minor child[ren] unless both Clients agree, and the child[ren]'s therapist and neutral child specialist, if any, approves.

FULL DISCLOSURE

The Clients agree to make such full and candid exchange of information as is necessary to make a proper evaluation of the case. Full disclosure of the nature, extent, value of, and all developments affecting: the client's income, assets and liabilities; and all other relevant matters is required. [Full disclosure of all relevant information relating to the Clients' children is also required.] Any material change in information previously provided must be promptly updated. The Clients authorize their respective lawyers to fully disclose all information which in the lawyer's judgment must be provided to the Collaborative Team in order to fulfill this commitment.

No formal discovery procedures will be used unless specifically agreed to in writing. However, the Clients may be required to sign a sworn statement making full disclosure of their income, assets and debts (a sworn inventory and appraisement). Affidavits may be utilized to confirm specific matters, such as the unavailability of certain information, or the existence or non-existence of documents or tangible things.

We shall maintain a high standard of integrity and shall not take advantage of each other or of known mistakes, errors of fact or law, miscalculations or other inconsistencies, but shall identify and correct them.

Collaborative Law Process Participation Agreement (Rev. 3/07)
© Collaborative Law Institute of Texas, Inc. 2004

CONFIDENTIALITY

In accordance with the Texas Family Code, the Clients agree to maintain the confidentiality of all oral and written communications relating to the subject matter of the case made by the Clients or the Collaborative Team, whether before or after the institution of formal judicial proceedings. The Clients agree that all oral communication and written material in the collaborative law process will only be admissible or discoverable if it is admissible or discoverable independent of the collaborative law process. This paragraph does not apply to reports of abuse or neglect required by law, agreed formal discovery, sworn documents prepared in this matter, a fully executed collaborative law settlement agreement or evidence of fraud.

A client and/or his or her collaborative lawyer is free to disclose all information to a lawyer hired to render a second opinion for that client in the collaborative law process or to that client's successor collaborative lawyer. In the event the collaborative law process is terminated, a client and/or his or her collaborative lawyer are free to disclose all information to that client's litigation lawyer.

This provision does not prohibit disclosure by a member of the Collaborative Team of case information for educational purposes without disclosing the identities of the Clients, nor does it prohibit participation by the Clients or either of them in educational forums or media interviews to discuss the collaborative law process.

OTHER LEGAL OPINIONS

Neither client shall consult a litigation lawyer about this matter so long as the collaborative law process continues, except for the limited purpose of obtaining a private opinion as to the potential outcome of the case in an adversarial proceeding. If at any time in the past twelve months or during the collaborative law process a client privately secures an opinion about this matter from another lawyer, including a litigation lawyer, the client agrees to disclose the identity of such lawyer to the Collaborative Team. If the opinion was sought prior to the signing of this Participation Agreement, then the client represents that the identity has been disclosed to the Collaborative Team before this Participation Agreement was signed. If the opinion is sought during the collaborative law process, the client agrees to disclose the identity before the client's initial consultation with the lawyer and promptly inform the Collaborative Team of the occurrence of each consultation the client has with such lawyer.

The client should give any lawyer offering an opinion on an issue(s) all information necessary to give informed advice, including reports of consultants whose services have been engaged in the collaborative law process. The Clients agree the work product and opinion of such privately engaged lawyer are attorney-client privileged and are not required to be disclosed in the collaborative law process.

The Clients agree a lawyer privately engaged to offer an opinion, and any other lawyer associated in the practice of law with that lawyer, are not disqualified from testifying as a fact or expert witness pertaining to attorneys' fees and are not prohibited from representing the consulting client in an adversarial proceeding between the Clients.

If both Clients jointly seek a second opinion from a lawyer then the opinion is to be disclosed to the Collaborative Team, and the lawyer is to be considered a neutral expert and is disqualified from testifying as a fact or expert witness in an adversarial proceeding between them and is prohibited from representing either of them in an adversarial proceeding between the Clients.

The Clients agree the work product, opinions, mental impressions, and the facts upon which they are based, of a consulted lawyer are not discoverable and are inadmissible in an adversarial proceeding regarding the case or in any other adversarial proceeding between the Clients, unless the Clients, the collaborative lawyers and consulted lawyer agree otherwise in writing.

AGREEMENTS

The Clients may agree to the entry of temporary orders. Upon request of either client or as required by local rules, the Code of Conduct set out in Exhibit "A" attached hereto shall be filed with the court as mutual injunctions. Further, whether entered as injunctions or not, the Clients agree to abide by the terms of Exhibit "A" until it is modified by court order or written agreement. The Code of Conduct and a fully executed Collaborative Law Settlement Agreement are contracts between the Clients and may be the basis for a claim against the client violating their terms in the event of termination of this process. In the event enforcement is sought, the collaborative lawyers shall withdraw.

Any partial or final written agreement, which is signed by both Clients and their respective collaborative lawyers, may be filed with the court as a collaborative law settlement agreement and may be made the basis of a court order. The Clients and the collaborative lawyers shall cooperate in preparing the documents necessary to effectuate the Clients' agreement. A collaborative lawyer may require the preparation and execution of all closing documents necessary to complete the case before entry of judgment. Either or both collaborative lawyers shall be permitted to appear in court to have agreed judgment(s) entered.

LEGAL PROCESS

Suspension of Court Intervention. The Clients and the collaborative lawyers agree that court intervention shall be suspended while the Clients are using the collaborative law process. Seeking court intervention for a judicially-imposed decision regarding an issue in the case automatically terminates the process.

No motion or document will be prepared or filed which would initiate court intervention, other than a [joint] Petition [for Divorce/to Modify Prior Order/other matter] [and an Answer]. If necessary, service of citation will be accepted by the Clients' respective lawyers. No hearing shall be set thereafter, other than to enter agreed orders and judgments.

Termination by Client. A client who has decided to terminate the collaborative law process shall notify his or her collaborative lawyer in writing. That client's collaborative lawyer shall then give prompt written notice to the other client through his or her collaborative lawyer and to the court. Upon notice of termination of the collaborative law process to the other collaborative lawyer, there will be a 30-day waiting period (unless there is an emergency) before a court hearing to permit each client to engage another lawyer and make an orderly transition.

If a client chooses to terminate the collaborative law process by seeking court intervention for a judicially-imposed decision, both collaborative lawyers shall withdraw. Neither collaborative lawyer (including any lawyer associated in the practice of law with the collaborative lawyer) may serve as a litigation lawyer on behalf of a client in this case or in any other matters between the Clients thereafter (other than a suit to enforce payment of the lawyer's fees). Each collaborative lawyer will cooperate in transferring the file.

Termination by Collaborative Lawyer. The collaborative law process must be terminated if a client engages in any of the following behaviors and persists in doing so after counseling by the client's collaborative lawyer:

1. refuses to disclose information, including the existence of documents, which in the collaborative lawyer's judgment must be provided to the other client or the Collaborative Team;
2. answers dishonestly any inquiry made by a client or member of the Collaborative Team;
3. takes an action that results in compromising the integrity of the process; or
4. fails or refuses to take an action which failure or refusal compromises the integrity of the process.

Under any of these circumstances, if the offending client refuses to terminate the collaborative law process, each client acknowledges that his/her respective collaborative lawyer has a duty to terminate the collaborative law process on behalf of the client, and by signing this agreement, each client authorizes his/her collaborative lawyer to terminate the collaborative law process by written notice to the Collaborative Team.

Withdrawal of Lawyer. If the collaborative law process is terminated, both collaborative lawyers shall immediately withdraw. If there is no termination of the collaborative law process, either collaborative lawyer may withdraw unilaterally by giving three days' written notice to his or her client and the other collaborative lawyer, unless substituted by a successor collaborative lawyer in which case no such notice is required. Notice of withdrawal of a collaborative lawyer does not necessarily terminate the collaborative law process; however, in order for the collaborative law process to continue, the client whose collaborative lawyer has withdrawn must engage a new collaborative lawyer who will agree in writing to be bound by this Participation Agreement. If the client whose collaborative lawyer has withdrawn chooses to represent himself or herself, the collaborative law process terminates and the other collaborative lawyer must withdraw.

REPRESENTATION AS TO PROPERTY

The final documents reflecting the Clients' financial settlement may include the following, or similar provisions, if either client requests the inclusion thereof:

Representations and Disclosures. The Clients represent to each other that the property listed represents all of the property in which either of them may have an interest.

Separate Property. Any property which is not listed or described and which is later determined to be the separate property of a client shall be and remain the separate property of that client.

Property and Liabilities Mistakenly Omitted. Any mistakenly omitted property which is not listed or described and is later determined to be the community property of the Clients, shall be subject to future division by the court. Any mistakenly omitted liabilities which are later determined to have been the joint liabilities of the Clients shall be subject to future allocation by the court.

Property and Liabilities Intentionally Omitted. Any community assets later determined to have been intentionally and fraudulently undisclosed by a client are set aside 100% to the other client. Any liabilities determined to have been intentionally and fraudulently undisclosed by a client are allocated 100% to the client who incurred the liability.

MEDIATION

Prior to termination of the collaborative law process, the Clients agree to give serious consideration to participation in mediation with a mediator who has received training in the collaborative law process.

PROFESSIONAL FEES

The Clients understand that the Collaborative Team members are entitled to be paid for their services. The Clients agree to make funds available from their community or separate estates, as needed, to pay these fees. The Clients understand that, if necessary, one client may be asked to pay all fees (including fees of the other client's lawyer) from community property managed solely by him or her (e.g., his or her salary) or from separate funds. The Clients agree that, to the extent possible, all fees and expenses incurred by both clients shall be paid in full prior to entry of a final judgment. Nonpayment of fees is cause for withdrawal by a Collaborative Team member, but not for a termination of the collaborative law process.

USE OF INTERNS AND COLLABORATIVE PROFESSIONALS AS OBSERVERS

The Clients agree that interns and collaborative professionals may observe one or more joint meetings in this collaborative law process, provided the observers agree to sign a written observation agreement preserving the confidentiality of any such observed meeting. The observer will not participate in the joint meetings except as an observer. Such observing shall be at no charge to the Clients.

UNDERSTANDINGS

The Clients understand that each collaborative lawyer is independent from the other and each represents and is an advocate for his or her client only in the collaborative law process. No attorney-client relationship is created between one client's collaborative lawyer and the other client by entering into this Participation Agreement or the collaborative law process. No legal duty, by contract or otherwise, is owed to a client by the other client's collaborative lawyer.

The Clients acknowledge the following: There is no guarantee that the collaborative law process will be successful in resolving the matter. The collaborative law process cannot eliminate concerns about the differences that have led to the current conflict. The Clients are expected to assert their own interests and their respective collaborative lawyers will help each of them to do so. The collaborative law process, can involve intense good-faith negotiation, but best efforts will be used to create options that meet the interests of both clients. Compromise may be needed to reach a settlement of all issues. Although the likely outcome of a litigated result may be discussed, the threat of litigation will not be used.

The parties understand that by agreeing to this process, they are giving up certain rights, including the right to conduct formal discovery (other than sworn inventories and appraisements), the right to participate in adversarial court hearings, and other procedures provided by the adversarial legal system, unless the process is terminated. The terms of this Participation Agreement may be modified, in a manner consistent with Texas law, only by written agreement signed by the Clients and the collaborative lawyers. However, the prohibition against either collaborative lawyer or any lawyer associated with that collaborative lawyer representing their client in contested matters against the other client is irrevocable and may not be modified.

Both clients and their respective collaborative lawyers hereby agree to comply with the spirit and letter of this Participation Agreement. Both clients and their collaborative lawyers acknowledge that they have read this Participation Agreement, understand its terms and conditions, and agree to abide by them.

Signed on _____.

[FIRSTNAME1]
Street Address
City, State, Zip code
Email

[FIRSTNAME2]
Street Address
City, State, Zip code
Email

[LAWYER1]
Collaborative Lawyer for
    [FIRSTNAME1]
SBN #
Street Address
City, State, Zip code
Office Phone
Fax Number
Email
Paralegal's email

[LAWYER2]
Collaborative Lawyer for
    [FIRSTNAME2]
SBN #
Street Address
City, State, Zip Code
Office Phone
Fax Number
Email
Paralegal's email

EXHIBIT "A"
CODE OF CONDUCT

Either client may:

1. Make expenditures and incur indebtedness for reasonable and necessary living expenses for food, clothing, shelter, transportation, entertainment, education and medical care.

2. Make expenditures and incur indebtedness for reasonable lawyers' fees and consultants' fees and expenses in connection with this matter.

3. Make withdrawals from accounts in financial institutions only for the purposes authorized by this agreement.

4. Engage in acts, make expenditures, incur indebtedness, make investments, and acquire, sell and transfer assets, as is reasonable and necessary to the conduct of either client's usual investment activities, business and occupation, subject to all such activities being fully disclosed and accounted for to the other client.

The Clients agree not to:

1. Communicate with the other client in an offensive manner.

2. Place telephone calls without a legitimate purpose of communication.

3. Destroy, remove, conceal, encumber, transfer, or otherwise harm or reduce the value of the property of one or both of the clients.

4. Falsify any writing or record relating to the property of either client.

5. Damage or destroy the tangible property of one or both of the clients, including any   document that represents or embodies anything of value.

6. Tamper with the tangible property of one or both of the clients, including any document that represents or embodies anything of value, thereby causing monetary loss to the other client.

7. Sell, transfer, assign, mortgage, encumber, or in any other manner alienate any of the property of either client, whether personalty or realty, and whether separate or community, except as specifically agreed to in writing or as specified in this agreement.

8. Incur any indebtedness, including but not limited to borrowing against any credit line or unreasonably using credit cards or cash advances against credit or bank cards, except as specifically agreed to in writing, or as specified in this agreement.

9. Make withdrawals from any checking or savings account in any financial institution for any purpose, except as specifically agreed to in writing, or as specified in this agreement.

10. Spend any sum of cash in the possession or subject to the control of either client for any purpose, except as specifically agreed to in writing, or as specified in this agreement.

11. Withdraw or borrow in any manner for any purpose from any retirement, profit-sharing, pension, death, or other employee benefit plan or employee savings plan or from any individual retirement account or Keogh account, except as specifically agreed to in writing.

12. Enter any safe-deposit box in the name of or subject to the control of either client, whether individually or jointly with others, unless the Clients accompany each other and jointly enter the box for the sole purpose of inventorying or dividing its contents by mutual agreement.

13. Withdraw or borrow in any manner all or any part of the cash surrender value of life insurance policies on the life of either client, except as specifically agreed to in writing.

14. Change or in any manner alter the beneficiary designation on any pension, retirement plan or insurance policy, except as specifically agreed to in writing.

15. Cancel, alter, fail to renew or pay premium, permit to lapse or in any manner affect or reduce the value of the present level of coverage of any life, disability, casualty, automobile, or health insurance policies insuring the Clients' property or persons, except as specifically agreed to in writing.

16. Change any provisions of any existing trust or will or execute a new trust or will without the prior written consent of the other client.

17. Terminate or in any manner affect the service of water, electricity, gas, telephone, cable television, or other contractual services, such as security, pest control, landscaping, or yard maintenance, at the residence of the other client or in any manner attempt to withdraw any deposits for service in connection with those services, except as specifically agreed to in writing.

18. Exclude the other client from the use and enjoyment of his or her respective residence.

19. Enter or remain on the premises of the residence of the other client without the other's consent.

20. Open or divert mail addressed to the other client, except as specifically agreed to in writing.

21. Sign or endorse the other client's name on any negotiable instrument, check, or draft, such as tax refunds, insurance payments, and dividends, or attempt to negotiate any negotiable instrument payable to the Clients or the other client without the personal signature of the other client.

22. Take any action to terminate or limit credit or charge cards in the name of the Clients or the other client, except as specifically agreed to in writing.

23. Transfer balances between credit cards or open new credit card accounts, except as specifically agreed to in advance in writing by the Clients.

24. Pay more than the [outstanding balance OR $_____ per month OR minimum monthly balance] owed on a credit card or charge account, except as specifically agreed to in writing.

25. Take any action to freeze or put a hold on any account with any financial institution from which the other client has the right to withdraw funds for purposes consistent with the authorizations contained in this agreement.

26. Operate or exercise control over the motor vehicles in the possession of the other client, except as specifically agreed to by the Clients.

27. Discontinue or reduce the withholding for federal income taxes on either client's wages or salary, except as specifically agreed to in writing.

28. Destroy, dispose of, or alter any financial records of the Clients, including but not limited to records from financial institutions (including canceled checks and deposit slips), all records of credit purchases or cash advances, tax returns, and financial statements.

29. Destroy, dispose of, or alter any relevant e-mail or other electronic data, whether stored on a hard drive or on a diskette or other electronic storage device.

30. Conduct surveillance of the other client's activities, including accessing the other client's emails, computer files and voice mail messages, and including the use of an investigator, detective or other individual paid for or engaged by a client or third party, or use of electronic listening or tracking devices, until this collaborative law process is terminated.

31. Engage the services of a stand-by litigation lawyer so long as the collaborative law process continues, except for the limited purpose of giving a second opinion in accordance with the provisions of this agreement set out in "Other Legal Opinions."

32. Exercise any stock options and warrants except as specifically authorized in advance by written agreement of the Clients.

33. Exercise any general or limited power of attorney, whether or not recorded, granted by one client to the other[optional: , except for directives to physicians, living wills, health care or medical powers of attorney, and HIPAA releases] .

34. Pay any indebtedness owed by the Clients or either of them prior to the date the indebtedness is due, unless agreed to specifically in writing by the Clients.

35. Create or contribute to, or reduce the value of or withdraw from or terminate, any trust of any kind or nature except as specifically authorized in advance by written agreement of the Clients.

36. Make any gift of any kind or nature, other than usual and customary gifts to family members of either client or mutual friends or their child(ren).

37. Create or contribute to any uniform gifts/transfers to minor act accounts or any trust of any kind or nature, except as specifically agreed to in advance in writing by the Clients.

38. File any extension or form with the Internal Revenue Service with regard to federal tax liability for any years of the marriage that limits the other client's choice of filing status, unless agreed to in advance in writing by the Clients.

39. File any federal income tax return or amendment to any federal income tax return for any year of the marriage during the pendency of the matter without first providing a true and correct copy of such proposed return to the lawyer of record for the other client at least 14 days in advance of the proposed tender to the Internal Revenue Service. This shall apply whether or not such filing is proposed to be by electronic methods or hard copy filing.

Goals Worksheet

Prior to the negotiation process: 1. Identify what you want and what needs would be satisfied if you receive what you say you want; 2. Use your best efforts to predict what you believe the other person will want and the needs that would be satisfied if the other person receives what he or she wants; and 3. Answer the following basic questions to help prepare yourself and your lawyer for the negotiation process:

What are the five most important goals you would like to accomplish during the collaborative law process?

(1)

(2)

(3)

(4)

(5)

Collaborative Law Process Participation Agreement (Rev. 3/07)
© Collaborative Law Institute of Texas, Inc. 2004

Why are these goals important to you or your family?

For Goal 1:

For Goal 2:

For Goal 3:

For Goal 4:

For Goal 5:

Putting yourself in the other person's shoes, what are the five most important goals that you believe he or she would most like to accomplish during the collaborative law process?

(1)

(2)

(3)

(4)

(5)

Putting yourself in the other person's shoes, as to each of the items listed above, explain why you believe these goals are important to the other person.

For Goal 1:

For Goal 2:

For Goal 3:

For Goal 4:

For Goal 5:

What are your five biggest concerns or worries about this family law matter?

(1)

(2)

(3)

(4)

(5)

For each concern or worry listed, why are you worried or concerned?

    For Concern 1:

    For Concern 2:

    For Concern 3:

    For Concern 4:

    For Concern 5:

From the perspective of the other person, what do you believe are his or her five biggest concerns or worries?

    (1)

    (2)

    (3)

    (4)

    (5)

From the perspective of the other person, for each concern or worry listed, why do you believe he or she is worried or concerned?

For Concern 1:

For Concern 2:

For Concern 3:

For Concern 4:

For Concern 5:

What goals do you have for your child(ren) after your family law matter is concluded?

(1)

(2)

(3)

(4)

(5)

What goals do you have regarding your relationship with the other person after your family law matter is concluded?

(1)

(2)

(3)

(4)

(5)

What are your concerns and worries about the negotiating process?

(1)

(2)

(3)

(4)

(5)

Collaborative Law Process Participation Agreement (Rev. 3/07)
© Collaborative Law Institute of Texas, Inc. 2004

What would be your concerns and worries about having to go to court to resolve the issues if the matter is not resolved by a collaborative law settlement agreement?

(1)

(2)

(3)

(4)

(5)

Printed in the United States
By Bookmasters